THE GROWTH HACKER'S

GUIDE TO THE GALAXY

100 PROVEN GROWTH HACKS
FOR THE DIGITAL MARKETER

MARK HAYES AND JEFF GOLDENBERG

THE GROWTH HACKER'S GUIDE TO THE GALAXY

100 Proven Growth Hacks for the Digital Marketer

Mark Hayes and Jeff Goldenberg

Published in the United States by Insurgent Publishing, LLC. PO Box 8043, Aspen, CO 81612

www.insurgentpublishing.com

ORDERING INFORMATION:

Insurgent Publishing books are available at special discounts for bulk purchases for sales promotions or corporate use. Special editions, including personalized covers, excerpts of existing books, or books with corporate logos, can be created in large quantities upon request. For more information, please contact the publisher by email at admin@ insurgentpublishing.com.

Although every precaution has been taken to verify the accuracy of the information contained herein, the author and publisher assume no responsibility for any errors or omissions. No liability is assumed for damages that may result from the use of information contained within.

Library of Congress Control Number: 2015959137

ISBN 978-1-940715-03-2 paperback

THANK YOU'S

A lot of people helped this book turn from dream into reality, and we want to take the opportunity to thank everyone:

A special thanks to Tom Morkes and Insurgent Publishing for guiding us so patiently through the process of writing a book. We originally learned about you through your email course on how to self-publish a book. By the end of your 7-day course, we knew we wanted you to publish our book. Thanks for everything.

Thanks to Sam Mallikarjunan for supporting our book and writing our foreword. You guys at HubSpot rock.

Thanks to the awesome founders and marketers who shared their amazing growth stories with us. Your candor, honesty and willingness to really mentor our readers is greatly appreciated. So thanks to Anum Hussain, Marie Nicola, Rob Walling, Hana Abaza, Aaron Houghton, Ethan Song, Brian Cristiano, Matt Epstein and Craig Miller.

Thanks to the people who really supported us back when we were only a little blog post: Sean Ellis, Dan Norris, Nicole Elizabeth DeMeré, Mark Evans, Massimo Chieruzzi and the Inbound.org community. Thanks to Jonathan Templeman for the kickass artwork.

MARK HAYES WOULD LIKE TO THANK:

Thank you to my mum, my brother Grant and his wife Vanessa and my niece. To all my staff Graham, Ben, Alfred, Becky, Talaina King, Petra, Jana, Ilya and many others that where able to help me during the writing of this book.

To all of supporters on Kickstarter for their patience during the writing of this book which took a lot longer than we thought.

Most of all to my girlfriend Maria, for being the most amazing woman that I have ever met.

JEFF GOLDENBERG WOULD LIKE TO THANK:

Thank you to all my friends and colleagues who have taught me along the way and put up with my curiosity and questions.

Thank you to my family – Sage, Jackson, Mom, Dad, Neil, Vanessa and little Caroline. I love you all.

Thank you to my Uncle Jack and Aunt Sandy – the original entrepreneurs. And to Pete and Kim (and Maddie!) for being the best.

Thank you to Graham O'Gallagher and Alfred Lee for helping me out when the going got tough. Hopefully I can repay you guys someday.

Thank you to Team Borrowell. You guys put up with all this book nonsense for so long and supported me along the way. What an awesome team to work with - you guys make me look good.

And most of all, we'd like to thank our backers on Kickstarter. Your support was felt the entire time, and your positive feedback kept us going when the going got tough. Thank you to Anthony Thomas, Tom Mo, Valerie Fox, Ronald Goldenberg, Jeremy Choi, Aaron Houghton, Russell Smith, David Bartholomeusz, Gino Santos, Peter Ferrante, Matt Zemon, Bartolome Bordallo, Skywalker Payne, Evan Shofron, Ramona Kirsch, Nicholas Norfolk, Aleksi Haapajoki, Neil Goldenberg, Bart Van De Kooij, Karen Hogg, Saumil Patel, Justin McGill, Rob Langer, Kevin, Anson Zeall, Andy Fuller, Mike van Hoenselaar, Jeffrey Stukuls, Bruce Brodeen, Jim Simisakakis, Kevin Kermes, Rick Rasmussen, Mark, Paresh Desai, Mohit Pawar, Philippe Le Roux, Peter Wright, Elizabeth Butterworth, Andrew Graham, Rick Martin, Jascha Jabes, Graham, Richard English, Rob Walling, Steve Daar, Arnie Malham, Filippo Campedelli, Alessandro Gargiulo, Caroline Rouben, Brian Teeney, Aubrey Jesseau, Nick Dellis, Matt Chatters, Raul Cristian Aguirre, Jason 'Beatdown Jr' Beaton, Mike Mason, Justin Jones, Kristina Johnson, Scott D. Brooks, Aron Lindegård, Curtis Priest, Avery Swartz, Peter, Doug, Euan Callus, Jon Grant, UrbanExplorer.com, Pavel Smirnov, Hristian Kambourov, Lennart Pilon, Matthew Doering, Geoff Cook, Derek Murphy, Isa Al Zeera, Kiwi Carranza, Jason Smith, Travis Scott Collier, Dim McNami, Kevin Tamming, Robert Clarke, Andrew Witchell, Robert, Samuel Hellman, Volker Holloh, Tim Chan King To, Ian Clifford, Domenic Mantella, Rob Palumbo, Parker 'Tmwsiy' Harrington, Luke Marshall, Leigh Pember, Natalino Picone, Karen Sergeant, Vinay, Geoff Marcy, Sanjay Nasta, Milen Kisov, Predrag Lesic, Don, Christy Campbell, Tommy Andorff, Travis Chambers, Haresh Patel, Jeremy O'Krafka, Jane Kearns, Diego Remus, Konrad Caban, Preben Frenning, David Wilson, Sander van Den Broek, Stephen Yee, Hans van Gent, Tyler, Murat Tortopoglu, Michael Schwanzer, Mark Rosenzweig, Fili Wiese, Bob, Rafa, Michael Casely-Hayford, Alin Vlad, Huge Shoe Sale, Lonn Shulkin, Marco Petkovski, Brady, Jennifer Cullenbine, Adam Tomat, Gavin Baker, Tessier, Candra M, Robert Williger, Victor Henning, Jeff Schnurr, Marcos Lavorato, Derek Morin, Thomas, Ross Simmonds, Greig Cranfield, Bill Birss, Marius S. Eriksrud, Warren Croce, Eva, Peter Hellerfelt, Vince Ferraro, Markus Sommer, Jason Ladd, Fae Daunt, Andy Frank, Filippo Toso, Murray Priestley, David Haskins.

A FINAL NOTE OF THANKS TO ZAPHOD BEEBLEBROX THE IV. WE WISH YOU WERE ALIVE TO READ THIS BOOK, BUT YOUR SPIRIT LIVES ON.

CONTENTS

PRODUCT MARKET FIT

TRANSITIONING TO GROWTH

CONTENTS

CONTENTS

SCALING FOR GROWTH

PERSONAL PRODUCTIVITY HACKS

"THE WORLD HAS MOVED ON."

That line, repeated throughout Stephen King's classic fantasy series "The Dark Tower," has been on my mind frequently while talking with the authors of the book you're about to read. In the series, it refers to the fact that fundamental forces that used to be taken for granted (such as distance over land and the passage of time) are no longer the set and certain boundaries of the world in which they live.

Today's transformations in business and commerce are no less significant. The characteristics that made incumbent businesses stable and valuable in the past are becoming less important -- and often actually making it more likely that they'll be disrupted. Institutional inertia -- the fact that businesses at rest tend to stay at rest until acted upon by an outside nerd-in-a-basement -- has poorly positioned modern leading firms to handle the rigors of "Big Bang" disruptive innovation.

In the June 2014 issue of the Harvard Business Review, authors Clay Christensen and Max Wessel (who pioneered much of the most compelling framework research on disruptive innovation), penned a piece that they called "The Capitalist's Dilemma." In it, they dispel the common strategic business assumption that -- above all -- capital is scarce and must be used as efficiently as possible. They cite a Bain & Company study estimating that "total financial assets are today almost 10 times the value of the global output of all goods and services." Rather than over-emphasize efficient allocation of capital above all else (a focus that they claim "has risen almost to the level of a religion"), investing in various frameworks of innovation, such as growth mechanisms for sustaining innovation, are a use of capital more likely to result in the long-term survival and growth of an organization.

Also, as also evidenced by whom we consider the "World's Best CEOs," solving for profitability has become less important than solving for enterprise growth. Jeff Bezos isn't widely considered one of the greatest CEOs in the world because of how profitable Amazon.com is (in fact, they rarely post impressive quarterly profit numbers), but rather because he's led Amazon to incredible sustained growth over time.
"Shareholder return" isn't measured as exclusively in dividends as much as in the ability of the company to grow in value and therefore grow the value of the stock. Simply put: The best executives empower their organizations with a charter mission to grow in value as quickly as possible.

This has led to many interesting developments, such as the rising supremacy of customer-centric unit economics. SaaS companies and other technology start-ups are no longer as concerned with net transactional revenue as they are in market share and their ability to out-leverage competitors in growth by focusing instead on customer acquisition and retention over time.

How necessary is this investment in growth above all? Many of the traditionally top place companies on lists such as the Fortune 1000 are being displaced by organizations that are growing more rapidly.

Keystone firms and companies that have survived and thrived for decades are being displaced by startups whose strategic advantage lies almost solely in their ability to outgrow incumbents and other competitors. Just because a company has survived the last 100 years does not at all guarantee that it will survive the next ten.

Building a culture of growth within an organization or team is just as important as the technical ability to execute growth campaigns. Because they've become so sophisticated, marketers and entrepreneurs often have a difficult time avoiding distractions. If you have the right people on your team and you've clearly communicated the key goals and performance indicators, there's rarely a shortage of good ideas to test. The harder thing to do is to keep the team focused and encourage them to ignore "fascinating distractions" while they invest their time and effort in testing metrics they can impact with statistical significance.

"Innovation" as a jargon term has become almost an intolerable business cliché. Hearing "We just need to innovate more" from a manager or executive is enough to spark furtive glances combined with exasperated eye rolls in any number of organizations. Growth and innovation are mind-sets, true, and to an extent they have to arise from a structure and culture that's nurtured from the highest executive levels.
However, in order for growth and innovation to actually occur and make an impact on the business, employees and teams need a structure and framework that directs and guides their efforts in a way that will drive the most value for the business.

That, along with the specific methods and frameworks you can use to drive growth, are what I hope for you to take from this book by these excellent authors.

The Charge of the Growth Brigade:
Data to right of them,
Data to left of them,
Data in front of them,
Count'd and number'd;
Measur'd models with massive growth,
Boldly they test and see,

Unto the laws of math,
With statistical significance be,
More value for their customers.

Sam Mallikarjunan
Head of Growth, HubSpot Labs

Introduction

What's that? "Yet another compendium of Atari-era marketing tactics!" we hear you softly groan to yourself.

"Aren't there enough guides on growth hacking floating about the internet already?", you then rightfully ask aloud. "There's blah and blah and blah, and then there's also blah, blah, blah". Agreed. No, really, we know that and – just like you – we've read most of them.

But where is all the cool new s@#t?

But you know what? After pouring over far too many blog posts and needlessly shoveling through various resources created by an ever-growing cadre of 'growth hack3rz', we got sick of coming across the "same ole', same ole'" examples.

Just because Hotmail did something considered to be a marketing "hack" in the 90s doesn't mean that it is just as relevant in today's cut-throat startup world saturated with SaaS startups of every which flavor.

What about all of the new and shiny tactics that cutting-edge marketers are using to blaze today's growth hacking trails? Or, to put it another way: "where is all of the cool new s@#t?" As it turns out, scattered across the far (and not so far) reaches of the startup blogosphere.

The quest for the 'Growth Hacking Holy Grails'

After doing some further digging through the digital startup catacombs, we realized that there is no single, regularly-updated resource of startup marketing hacks.

So, as any true entrepreneurial type would do, we decided that this is not good enough. It was time to launch our own quest for the 'Growth Hacking Holy Grails' out there!

Launch said quest we did and the result is this collection of modern growth hacks and growth hacking case studies. Our aim was to complement the more established resources already available and, if you're a die-hard Growth Jedi Master, then you may have seen these hacks referenced elsewhere. However, the format that we've adopted will still make for worthwhile and educational reading.

How's that for a double cheese pizza?

PRODUCT MARKET FIT

Disclaimer

And while we don't make any claims that using the hacks in this book will turn
a startup marketing Michael Jordan, our hope is that you'll at least be able to s
three-pointers by the time you've gone through it.

Now lace-up your standard-issue startup founder flip-flops (we know you can'
Air Jordans yet), it's game time!

So before we embark on this intergalactic voyage to growth hacking greatness, we should start by explaining how the Guide is organized.

The Guide is divided into three sections, based on Sean Ellis' (the Godfather of Growth) Startup Pyramid model of 1) Product/Market Fit 2) Transition to Growth and 3) Growth

In the first section, Product/Market Fit, we are going to explore some growth hacks that will help you QUICKLY and CHEAPLY ensure that you're selling something your customers want.

Now that may sound simple, but Product/Market Fit is the Bermuda Triangle of startups, where most startups go to die. According to startup expert Steve Blank "Customer Validation proves that you have found a set of customers and a market who react positively to your product". This is what you're looking for.

While there are no growth hacking "silver bullets" that fit all startups, there is one piece of advice that applies to everyone on this voyage – do not growth hack until you have empirical evidence that proves you have achieved Product/Market Fit. Also called Traction, you're looking for what Gabe Weinberg defines as "quantitative evidence of consumer demand".

So what does that look like? Sean Ellis suggests that at least 40% of your early users would say that they'd be "very disappointed" if they could no longer use your product. Until that point, the goal of the startup is to minimize your burn rate (the amount you spend each month to keep the lights on) and focus all available resources on customer development and product development to match your value proposition with your target consumer's needs.

Until that point, you're pouring money into the proverbial 'leaky bucket', and too much will trickle out to make your marketing efficient and scalable. While incredibly tempting for novice entrepreneurs and marketers, you're almost guaranteed to waste your valuable marketing dollars if you try to grow prematurely. The case studies in this section show examples of massive companies and how they ensured their own Product/Market Fit before accelerating their growth.

The tactics around Product/Market Fit are also outlined in this chapter. Start with intense customer development and talk to as many customers as you can to better understand their problems and see how you can be the solution. Make sure that you focus on a customer problem that is acute, that is important (often their #1 problem) and one that they're willing to spend money to solve. Oftentimes startups flounder by addressing a #2 or #3 need, or a need that isn't worth spending money to solve.

Once you have proof of Product/Market Fit, your task changes to focus on how to acquire customers efficiently enough to turn a profit. Tomasz Tunguz, VC at Redpoint Ventures, gives amazing recommendations in his article A Framework for Maximizing Startup Marketing Effectiveness. He describes the initial startup goal is to "find a channel with profitable unit economics (where the cost-of-customer-acquisition is less than the gross margin over some lifetime-value estimate) with as small an investment as possible to minimize burn" – aka the Holy Grail of growth marketing. Tunguz goes on to explain that this is achieved by focusing on the bottom of the funnel (people ready to buy), experimenting with different tactics, learning quickly and focusing on direct-response advertising such as pay-per-click.

The growth hacks and case studies in this channel will help you achieve these goals.

Buckle your seat belts and prepare for launch!

01

THE LANDING PAGE HACK

How to validate any idea in under an hour.

THE PHASE:
Pre Launch

DIFFICULTY:
Easy

WE USE:
Unbounce.com
(free for 30 days,
then $49/month
for 5,000 visitors
per month)

The Hack: "Hello…hello? Snap out of it!" Yep, it's easy to sit back and imagine your latest, greatest idea becoming an overnight success. But before you start dreaming about being the next Angry Birds, maybe it's time you flew out your chair and out of the building!

That's right, outside. You know, where the customers are. Your job is to get out there and mingle, talk to them, listen to what they have to say and learn. Thankfully, with the Internet at your disposal, you don't physically have to pound the street anymore to gather opinions. That's what landing pages are for.

This hack will teach you how to quickly launch a landing page that will allow you to test your product concept, collect email addresses and gain valuable customer feedback. And when we say customers, we mean real customers. Asking your mom and sister doesn't count!

With a landing page, you can send customers to your site, ask for feedback, collect email addresses and validate your offering. You can even buy a little bit of traffic and test your concept in front of actual customers, and not just your mom.

Now Hack It:

- Start by getting your act together! Write down your value proposition, your target markets, your features and benefits and collect up your creative assets such as photos, videos and text. If you don't have good photos, visit startupstockphotos.com to get some.

- Set up a free account with Unbounce.

- Select a template based on your objectives for the site. For example, if you want to generate leads, use a template with a prominent lead generation form on the homepage, above the fold. If you're really picky (and sometimes you should be) you can browse through literally hundreds of templates for sale at ThemeForest.net. Choose a template which works for you aesthetically, suits the target market and matches the assets you've collected. If you don't have great imagery, don't select a photo-heavy template.

- Drag and drop. Use the landing page creator to customize every aspect of your page. Don't panic if this seems difficult at first. By the time you've customized your first template, you'll be a pro. And in the off chance you do hit a major roadblock, Unbounce has great customer service to sort you out.

- Buy a great website domain for your product and have them forward the domain (with masking) to your unique landing page link. That way, the landing page will look like your homepage and not a subdomain of Unbounce.

- All that's left is to start sending traffic and measuring! Measure click through rates and conversion rates from each traffic source. This may sound like a lot, but trust us, all this squirreling of data will come in handy later on.

PRO TIP:
Stop. Rebuild. Repeat. Once you've kicked off your first landing page, take some time to build a second version. Only this time, tweak a few variables. You could add a new value proposition, juggle around with the price or even just try out a snazzy new layout. Send 50% of your traffic to each version and see which one leads to more conversions (email addresses, signups, purchases etc.).

02

THE 'PIMP MY UNBOUNCE PAGE' HACK

How to add a video background to any Unbounce landing page

THE PHASE:
Pre Launch

DIFFICULTY:
Advanced

WE USE:
Unbounce.com
(free for 30 days,
then $49/month
for 5,000 visitors
per month)

The Hack: We know what you want! You want a landing page that looks like it just landed from "Planet Awesome" don't you? Well, you're in luck. We've got just the right hack to make your Unbounce landing page look like a fancy, expensive website.

Landing pages with video backgrounds are super popular these days (thanks to companies like Airbnb, PayPal and Spotify). This expert hack will teach you how to add a video background to your landing page and give your business that "big league" swag.

We all want to launch our product with a beautiful, fully functional website. But those pesky lean start-up-type people keep insisting that we launch with a Minimum Viable Product. All so that before we break the bank building the product, we know for sure that customers like what we're building.

So anytime we can find a hack that makes our MVP look more professional, our ears perk up. We're on board with any idea which lets us maintain a lean start-up launch while giving off that 'big league' aura.

Now Hack It:

- First you need a video. Either find a video on YouTube or upload your own video to YouTube.

- Get the code snippet from here.Don't freak out after reading "code snippet,"it's easy!

- Go into Unbounce page builder and click on Javascripts. Name your script anything you like, select "before body end tag" and paste the code snippet.

- Now you need to customize this code snippet line:

- lpVideoBG('#lp-pom-block-9', '2XX5zDThC3U', 560, 315, 0);

- as follows:

- lpVideoBG('#SectionID', 'YoutubeVideoID', width, height, muted);

- Now just add the page section ID where you want the video to appear, the YouTube ID for your video, the height and width you want for the video, and either "0" for sound or "1" to mute.

- Save your JavaScript changes.

PRO TIP:
Make sure you set a static background image as well. Forboth unsupported browsers or mobile users, the page will default to the static image and still look great.

03

THE HEADS-UP DISPLAY HACK

How to create a metrics dashboard that keeps you on top of your KPIs

THE PHASE:
Pre Launch

DIFFICULTY:
Intermediate

WE USE:
Ducksboard.
com (Free for 30
days and then
$19/month for 1
dashboard)

The Hack: They say you can't manage what you don't measure. We say, measuring is only half the battle. What you need is relevance. This hack will show you how to create a customized dashboard to measure and display your key performance indicators, and watch your bottom line grow.

Data is very fashionable right now. And like all things fashionable, it's fast becoming a real head turner for marketers. That's because now more than ever, there's heaps of data available for free. In fact, there's so much data available, that the novice marketer feels totally overwhelmed, and gets hit with the proverbial fire-hose as soon as they dip a toe into their marketing data.

The trick to overcome this feeling is simple. All you have to do is prioritize the 3 or 4 key performance metrics that are most important to your company. And, instead of getting intimidated attempting to track dozens of metrics, focus on the most important and track them obsessively.

Now Hack It:

- Sign up for a free account at ducksboard.com.

- Define which Key Performance Indicators are the most important and need to be monitored. This will vary based on your industry. The most common areas to focus on are

    - Funnel Statistics - website visitors, conversion rates, cost per acquisition, sales

    - Social Statistics - followers, growth, mentions

    - Site Performance - SEO, landing pages, blog

    - Project Management - integrate Basecamp or Trello to keep track of projects

- Use the existing library of integrations to connect your accounts to Ducksboard. Most times, you only need to provide your login credentials or an API key that's readily available

- Start with just the most important KPIs and build out from there. Keep it simple, and get in the rhythm of tracking your KPIs.Don't get frustrated with the integrations; some take a few hours to track results. And if all else fails, use Ducksboard support to help you get connected.

PRO TIP:
You can keep your entire team on the same page by displaying your Ducksboard on a TV on your office wall. Having your entire team following the same KPIs can be a big factor in creating a culture of growth.

04

THE CAC HACK

How to benchmark your cost per acquisition target, so you know how much to spend per customer

THE PHASE:
Pre Launch

DIFFICULTY:
Easy

WE USE:
Just our minds!

The Hack: If you've spent any time raising VC financing or studying SaaS marketing, you've definitely heard of Cost Per Acquisition or CPA. Your CPA is the amount of money you spend to acquire a new customer.

With this simple hack to calculate your target CPA, you'll never have to spend $50 to acquire a customer who's only worth $20!

Growth Hackers live and breathe their Cost Per Acquisition (sometimes referred to as CAC, because it stands for Cost to Acquire a Customer, and is just fun to say!).We use it to compare marketing channels, to compare campaigns within a channel, and to evaluate marketing opportunities.

It's the lifeblood for growth hackers, because we're always aiming to acquire customers efficiently, affordably and cheaper than our competitors. By maniacally tracking CPA, you can ensure that you're focusing on marketing channels that not only generate customers, but generate profitable customers.

CPA is also the umbilical cord between the marketing department and the company's bottom line.

Now Hack It:

- Sometimes the easiest hacks are the most important hacks!

- Estimate the lifetime value of your typical customer (LTV).If you have recurring revenue, estimate the number of cycles a customer will stay with you. Or estimate how many repeat purchases your typical customer will make. This number will change over time, as you replace estimates with actual data.

- Now that you know how much revenue a customer will generate over their relationship with you, use your margin calculation to estimate the lifetime profit of the customer. For example, if the LTV is $80 and you have 50% margins, your LTV profit is $40.

- Set your Cost Per Acquisition (CPA) ceiling, which is one third of your LTV profit. In the previous example, if your LTV profit is $40, your CPA ceiling is $40/3 or $13.33.

- Your CPA ceiling is the most you can spend to acquire a customer and still remain profitable and poised for growth. Growth hackers strive to drive their CPA down below the average cost of acquisition for their particular industry.

PRO TIP:
Many reputable thought leaders and consultants set their CPA ceiling at one third of the LTV revenue. This is too way much to spend; ignore these people. Instead, set your CPA ceiling off of LTV profit.

05

THE REAL
WORLD HACK

How to ensure that your product
solves a real customer problem

THE PHASE:
Pre Launch

DIFFICULTY:
Intermediate

WE USE:
Canvas free
at http://www.
businessmodel-
generation.com/
canvas/vpc - Buy
the book too!

The Hack: Ever hear the joke about the guy who invented the helicopter ejection seat? It never really took off! Yeah, we know that joke was lame. But you know what really isn't funny? Spending time and money to build a product no one wants.

To ensure you're never the butt of this kind of joke, we suggest prototyping your value proposition using Alex Osterwalder's Value Proposition Canvas. It will help ensure that your product or service is addressing an acute customer need.

Alex Osterwalder is most widely known for his creation of the Business Model Canvas - a tool and process that allows you to map out your company's business model and test it against other alternative models. His most recent book called "Value Proposition Design" builds on his canvas concept, but focuses on your value proposition, by ensuring that your product creates the "gain creators" and "pain relievers" that remove your customer's pains and enables your customer's gains.In simpler words, it ensures that your product fixes the main problem that your customer is experiencing.

By using this canvas, you can ensure that your product is a "must have" for your customers, before launching it into the market.

Now Hack It:

- Download the Value Proposition Canvas and (preferably) read Osterwalder's book, to understand how to populate the canvas.

- Start from the customer side and ask yourself the famous question "what job is my customer hiring my product to do"? This will force you to look at your product as the solution to your customer's problem. Brainstorm the pains that they're looking to solve and the gains they're hoping to achieve by using your product.

- Now focus on your product. How does your value proposition solve the customer's pains? How does your value proposition enable your customer's gains?

- Map the two canvases against each other and evaluate your product market fit hypothesis. Are you solving a problem that makes your product a "need to have"? If not, how can you better address the needs of your target customers?

PRO TIP:
You can download the first 100 pages of the book for free here:https://strategyzer. com/value-proposition-design. Also, their companion website has a ton of great videos and downloadable resources and shouldn't be skipped.

06

THE DECOY EFFECT HACK

How to use psychology to help determine your optimal product pricing

THE PHASE:
Pre Launch

DIFFICULTY:
Easy

WE USE:
Nothing

The Hack: What do we really know about what we want? Psychologists believe - not that much. And our minds can be easily tricked into choosing options that aren't often in our best interest. Sometimes these choices may even be detrimental to maximizing utility for us as consumers. For example, let's examine the concept of "value." Value is a relative term and, logically, it has no absolute worth. It's a proven fact that a "fair" price can be different for the same product or service depending on circumstances and context. As a growth hacker, you need to use this psychological loophole to maximize the perceived value of your SaaS subscription plans. Here's a neat hack to help you achieve this with minimal effort.

Now Hack It:

- Psychologists call it the "decoy effect" and it is a pricing hack than can really help you to increase sales of your premium plans, if done right.

- In fact, you would've seen it used in the pricing of many goods and services but probably never gave it too much thought.

- The basics of this pricing technique are that, instead of having two pricing plans - say, an entry-level one and a premium one - you add a third, "decoy" plan.

- Say, you charge $20 per month for your no-frills, starter plan and $50 per month for your everything-and-the-founder's-kitchen-sink one. The majority of your users will typically end up going with the starter plan. We're all cheap skates...

- By introducing a third "mid-tier" plan, you make the choice less obvious. Let's say, you price your new plan at $30 per month and allow users to gain access to most of the features of your premium plan, except couple.

- Now users are more likely to go with the mid-tier plan due to their having an additional comparison point. See, value IS a very relative concept.

- Try it, and watch your revenue grow...

- Still don't believe us? Next time you're in your local cafe, pay attention to which of the three cup sizes people usually tend to go with.

- Growth hacking is all around you!

07

THE TESTING HACK

How to conduct simple but effective A/B tests on your landing page

THE PHASE:
Pre Launch

DIFFICULTY:
Intermediate

WE USE:
Optimizely.com
(free account)

The Hack: A/B testing is like the cool fraternity on campus - everyone wants in. And if you hope to make it big in the start-up marketing world, you should want in too. That's because A/B testing has the potential to uncover extremely valuable customer feedback.

If you conduct just one A/B test per week, you'll accumulate the results of 50 tests over the course of a year, which could yield 12-15 significant improvements. Like always, the key to getting good is getting started.

A/B testing used to only be nerd cool - mostly IT people and coders. For the rest of us non-technical marketers, our thrills came simply from getting ONE website launched, let alone testing multiple versions.

Now companies such as Optimizely make A/B testing really simple to install, execute and analyze, creating opportunities for marketers to constantly experiment with their messaging, user interface, offer and much more.

Simply put, define an experiment by identifying an important website variable, create multiple website versions to test that variable, and split your traffic over the two test versions. Whichever version produces the better response...implement that one immediately and move on to the next test!

Now Hack It:

- Sign up for a free account at Optimizely.com

- Carefully follow the instructions to add the Optimizely code snippet to your website. This is very easy and only needs to be done the first time. From now on you'll be able to run experiments without touching your website's code.

- Create an A/B testing spreadsheet. Here you will keep a running list of hypotheses that you want to test.Keep the list prioritized, so the top test is the one you want to conduct next. This way you'll ensure that you're focused on the most promising hypothesis at all times.

- Use the Optimizely visual editor to set up the versions and create the test.Once you get a hang of the interface, this becomes incredibly easy. Determine how you're going to measure the performance - usually by defining a conversion and measuring the conversion rates (a sale, a completed lead form, a newsletter sign-up, an ebook download, etc.)

- Track your results and select a "winner" when the data is meaningfully better. Don't worry, Optimizely will clearly tell you which version performed better and whether the results were significant.

- Keep track of your results in your spreadsheet - this will become an exceedingly valuable reference as you execute tests.

PRO TIP #1:
It's estimated that 2-3 out of every 10 tests will results in a significant learning, so consistency is the key. If you run one test a week for an entire year (and assuming you're prioritizing the tests correctly), you'll run 50 tests a year and gain 12-15 meaningful results!

PRO TIP #2:
In a rush to make a quick website content change? You can use Optimizely as a quick editor. While it's not recommended to do often, as it adds unnecessary code to your website, it's a really quick method for updating your site in a pinch!

CASE STUDY #1
ETHAN SONG
CO-FOUNDER
AND CEO,
FRANK & OAK

Disrupting Apparel

Located in the cultural hotbed of Mile-End in downtown Montreal, Frank and Oak makes it ridiculously easy for men to look good. Founded in February 2012 by two childhood friends, Ethan Song and Hicham Ratnani, their mission is simple: help a generation of men dress and live well. Far from the typical e-commerce shop, Frank and Oak is changing the way men shop by integrating design and technology to offer outstanding clothes and accessories conveniently and at reasonable prices.

To ensure quality at every touchpoint, Frank and Oak is vertically integrated. Meaning they do everything independently, from designing the products to working closely with carefully selected manufacturers. According to Ethan, having this business model is the best way to ensure that the customer is receiving the products and experience that is right for them and inline with the brand. In short, Frank and Oak delivers the highest quality every single month with the greatest attention to detail.

Today, Frank and Oak has over two million members and ships over 1,000 packages a day. However, Ethan's initial traction goal was to have 10,000 pre-signups by the time it launched. The reason pre-signups were so important to Ethan was that it allowed each and every customer to have a very tailored experience. During the on-boarding process, users are prompted to answer questions related to their size, style preferences and overall lifestyle. The importance of this process according to Aaron was, "we can personalize the experience for you, which is important to us; we can send you products, we can send you content you can show your friends."

Before Ethan and Hicham's success with Frank and Oak, they owned another e-commerce clothing company, Modasuite. The vision behind this company was to offer men more choices and allow them to be in full control of their wardrobe. Simply put, Modasuite did custom shirting solving the fit problem for men. Despite good early traction and raising money with the company, Ethan knew something was missing. According to him, "we realized that men wanted simplicity. They didn't want something complicated, they wanted to save time, they wanted you to do all the work for them so they could enjoy their lives." This was a huge change from the current offering with Modasuite, but a necessary pivot to achieve product-market fit.

With a full 180 degree pivot from Modasuite to Frank and Oak, the team was tasked with acquiring 10,000 pre-signups for the impending February launch. With a simple landing page, here is how the team achieved their target:

Create a compelling Value Proposition

Most new founders overlook the importance of a clear and compelling value proposition as a source for growth. However, for Ethan getting the value proposition right and creating engaging stories around the brand was essential. All other activities stemmed from highly impactful messaging. For example, on the Frank and Oak landing page they created to collect signups was an eye-catching image with a simple tagline, "premium threads under $50." This simple, but intriguing tagline drove a lot of interest with people who resonated with the messaging. E-commerce fashion is becoming a saturated market, being able to cut through all the noise by communicating your value loudly with so few words is critical. Targeting online communities and posting the value proposition was a very successful tactic to driving pre-signups. Ethan posted the link to the landing page on Facebook groups and forums, and because the value proposition was convincing, people would be curious and want to sign up.

Empower members to drive growth

Everyone wants to rock social media, but so few people are actually able to do it in a way that drives significant value for their business. In order to drive people to the site, Ethan focused on incentivizing and engaging people t   hrough social media. One of the strategies used to do this, he leveraged relevant influencers he believed aligned with their values on social media platforms, who had over 100,000 followers to build momentum and credibility. Using influencers as a tool to help portray the brand's lifestyle image was a pivotal part of creating more meaningful engagement around its products.

Once people arrived at Frank and Oak's landing page, it was important to find a way to leverage new and existing members. To do this, a viral loop was built that would enable members to create more members through incentives. Ethan would measure how many people were signed up through referrals. People were incentivized to invite friends in order to get special promotions and early access to products. The more friends that would sign up, the better the incentives. Frank and Oak had a waiting list during pre-launch and for a few months after the launch. The only way to get early access was to invite more friends. This scarcity mentality drove huge viral growth for Frank and Oak.

Leverage existing relationships to build PR

Building PR momentum can be a big challenge for many founders who struggle with timing and getting coverage. For Ethan, the formula to getting PR is very simple. The first thing you need to have is a good story. This means that you need to be able to find different angles that make your product compelling as well as understand people's interests. As Ethan said, "there are trends in tech, and in some ways when you launch it's actually good to be aligned with the trend because then you are in-line with the topic people want to talk about." Ethan's main strategy with PR was to use existingrelationships as opposed to cold-calling and hustling people. The good old pound the pavement and send out cold pitches to media just does not work. Ethan reached out to a contact of his, who introduced him to a writer at TechCrunch. On launch day, without even seeing the website, an article was written about Frank and Oak. Once Ethan had the first article, he was able to use it to pitch other media which led to being featured in Time Magazine, The Next Web and several other news outlets. In Ethan's own words, "PR drives more PR."

Over a two month period from December until the launch in February, the Frank and Oak team acquired over 10,000 pre-signups. Over the first six months after launching, they were able to almost double business every two months.

When asked what key lessons Ethan wanted other marketers and founders to take away, he said:

First, use data to find product-market fit. Product-market fit has become a popular catchphrase, but determining when you have it and when you don't can be tricky for many entrepreneurs. As Ethan said, "it's only by having a product in the market, getting data, by testing it with customers, that we realized that the real value of our product was almost the opposite of our initial value offering." Without having launched a product and seeing how it responded in the market, Ethan would not have been able to find the product-market fit he did with Frank and Oak.

Second, create compelling stories that allow people to connect with the overall essence of your brand. People don't just buy products, they buy brands that align with their values. According to Ethan, the key to growing was creating content about the lifestyle they wanted to create as opposed to just selling the products. "Touching on the values behind the product is a much more powerful way of communicating the brand than to talk about the product."

Third, keep your approach flexible. Not every marketing channel will produce the results you are hoping for. It's important to keep an ear to the ground and remain responsive so you can adapt to changing trends in technology and customer behavior. The key is to adopt a flexible methodology so that you can measure and test it as soon as possible, and scale the channels that do produce the desired results

08

THE NAME GAME HACK

How to find the perfect name
for your product or service

THE PHASE:
Pre Launch

DIFFICULTY:
Easy

WE USE:
NamingForce.com
($250 for 800+
name ideas)

The Hack: Okay, so calling your company something like the FLDSMDFR (Flint Lockwood Diatonic Super Mutating Dynamic Food Replicator) isn't the best idea. In case you're wondering, that reference is from the Pixar film Cloudy with a Chance of Meatballs which is worth a watch for any budding entrepreneur. And if you're like most entrepreneurs, you've probably shopped around for branding agencies and been stuck with several thousand dollars' worth of sticker shock.

How about you try this first - spend $250 with this service to generate 800 different ideas for your product. Spend the thousands on ping pong tables and PlayStations instead!

But we also understand that coming up with a great name for a business or a product is really tough. Sometimes the name comes quickly and makes sense right away. Sometimes it takes hours and hours of brainstorming to come up with one, and you're still not confident it's the right one. And sometimes a bad name turns into a homerun, or a great name fails miserably.

But our quick fix solution to this is one word - crowdsourcing. We love crowdsourcing pretty much anything! You should too. Any time you get the chance to harness the power of the crowd to get a cost efficient result is a great deal. Also, before you spend thousands of dollars or hours, try Naming Force. They'll get you almost 1000 name ideas for $250.

Now Hack It:

- Launch a contest at NamingForce.com. Provide a really good brief about your product or service.

- Communicate with the "namers," giving them feedback on their results

- Naming Force then conducts some basic market research on all the names, finding out which are the most popular. They then provide you with a ranked list of all the name suggestions.

- Also included on that list are basic statistics on U.S. trademark availability and domain name availability. Pay attention to these columns to ensure that your preferred domain is available.

- Select a winner and Naming Force will pay the winning "namer." It's as simple as that

PRO TIP:
Sometimes a submitted name will give you the inspiration for an even better name. And sometimes a combination of multiple submitted names produces the best result. Be open minded and flexible, you never know where creative inspiration will come from.

09

THE TIM FERRIS LITMUS TEST HACK

How to use Google Adwords to test demand for your product

THE PHASE:
Pre Launch

DIFFICULTY:
Intermediate

WE USE:
Google AdWords

The Hack: In his hugely successful book "The Four Hour Workweek," Tim Ferris describes how to leverage a small spend on Google AdWords to find out if anyone wants your product BEFORE spending a lot of time and money launching it.It also generates awesome data on keyword performance, ad concepts and geography that will be invaluable later. If all this sounds yawn-worth, go ahead...skip it. But we bet you'll be back soon enough to re-read this chapter!

Tim Ferris calls this "micro-testing" which is the process of executing small, inexpensive tests - prior to launch - to see if customers respond to your offer.In the old days, entrepreneurs would use small display ads or classified ads in a targeted magazine.Today, Google obviously lets you target customers at the point of search, making it easier and better targeted.Tim calls the process Best-Test-Invest/ Divest. We'll explain below.

Now Hack It:

- Do some basic keyword research. Use Google's Keyword Planner tool to identify 50-100 keywords that have decent monthly traffic and affordable suggested cost per click (CPC).Later on, we'll teach you how to do more advanced keyword research.

- BEST: While searching these keywords, study your competitor's ads and create an offer that's more compelling than theirs.

- TEST: Create two different ads and test them on Google Adwords platform with a $50 daily budget. Use simple Google Analytics to track conversions, to determine which ad/keyword mix performed the best.

- INVEST OR DIVEST: Use this data to determine whether there is sufficient customer interest for your product BEFORE spending lots of time and money on it.

PRO TIP:
Some entrepreneurs use micro-testing long before they even have a product. This can be done in several ways: collect email addresses as your "conversion" and estimate the percentage that would actually purchase; Have the "submit order" button not process the sale, and tell them it's sold out; create an intermediate engagement step such as "refer a friend" and test the conversion; or develop a pre-order system, and only charge their credit card once the product ships.

10

THE 5 SECOND TEST HACK

How to watch customers interact with your website

THE PHASE:
Pre Launch

DIFFICULTY:
Easy

WE USE:
Usertesting.com
- 1 video free
through peek.
usertesting.com,
then $49
per video.

The Hack: Right, so we're about to suggest watching people do stuff. But we promise it won't be creepy at all. In fact, it's going to be beneficial for your business.UserTesting.com offers the ability to get videos of users (from within your target demographic) interacting with your website. You get to set up tasks for them, ask them questions and get their feedback - then watch the videos of them doing so minutes later. Warning - this can get very addictive!

But just so you know, watching users peruse your website and critique your business can be hard on the nerves. But this is quickly offset by the immediate feedback you receive, which can be quite exciting. UserTesting.com has a huge pool of website reviewers, who get paid to create user videos of themselves reviewing your website, completing your tasks answering your questions. While the testing audiences are obviously not engaged website users, their feedback can be extremely useful, if your website is less intuitive than you think.

Now Hack It:

- Start with a Peek! Peek is a free service, offered by UserTesting.com that allows you to get a free five-minute video review. Start here to understand how to create effective user testing tasks and questions.

- Then head over to UserTesting.com and buy a group of videos. Videos are $49 each, and we recommend doing at least five of them.

- Follow the wizard to create your user testing questions and tasks. Choose from their "most popular" tasks or create your own from scratch. The testers will follow your instructions as they navigate through your site. Launch the tests.

- Wait about an hour and your videos will be ready for review. They will include tester audio, plus video captured from their screen. If you asked written questions, they will also be available with the videos.

- Pay careful attention to places where the user has trouble using your site, as well as suggestions they have to make it better.

PRO TIP:
User testing your site with non-engaged users is a great way to ensure that your user experience and user interface are as easy as possible. If visitors are getting lost, figure out how to make your flow more simple.

11

THE FEEDBACK HACK

How to use Survey Monkey to collect customer feedback

THE PHASE:
Pre Launch

DIFFICULTY:
Easy

WE USE:
SurveyMonkey.
com (FREE up to
100 responses,
$29/month
unlimited)

The Hack: So, this isn't a new hack by any means. But everything worthwhile doesn't have to be shiny and new. Sometimes, old is gold. And this hack is certainly worth its weight in it. Survey Monkey allows you to create, circulate and analyze customer surveys, to find out what your customers REALLY need. This is very helpful in creating buyer personas. And if you don't want to or can't find the time to talk to customers, you should definitely find another line of work.

The start-up pros call it "customer development" and it is the most important (and most avoided) step in the start-up launch process. The process sounds simple - get out of the building, talk to customers, find out what problems they are having and then launch your product only if it solves their biggest problems. However, first time entrepreneurs have trouble speaking to customers. They are nervous to solicit feedback, they tend to ignore the negative, and they introduce their solution too quickly.

The easiest way to solicit customer feedback is through a well-planned survey, and Survey Monkey makes it simple. So take a deep breath, get your big boy pants on and start defining your target audience. Once you've done that, just start sending as many surveys out as you can.

Now Hack It:

- Sign up for a free account at SurveyMonkey.com.Upgrade to a paid account if you need more than 10 questions and 100 responses. The more the better, so long as you're surveying your precise target market.

- Select a simple template and create a survey using your own questions, or a database of popular questions that Survey Monkey provides.

- Don't ask too many questions or your response rate will lag. If a question doesn't promise to get you amazing insight, ditch it for one that does.

- Use email, social media or live interviews to solicit as many responses as possible. Anyone with your survey link can take the survey, they don't need to have an account.

- Watch the responses come in, analyze them using the simple reports, and export to Excel for later use.

PRO TIP #1:
First time entrepreneurs look for feedback that supports their hypotheses. Veteran entrepreneurs look for feedback that destroys their hypotheses, knowing that it's better to find out early. Focus on the negative data and figure out how to improve.

PRO TIP #2:
You can also buy survey response audiences, both through Survey Monkey's own audiences or by buying simple social media ads and targeting the correct audience.

12

THE INSTANT FEEDBACK HACK

How to use Qualaroo to collect instant, in situ feedback

THE PHASE:
Pre Launch

DIFFICULTY:
Intermediate

WE USE:
Qualaroo.com
(14 days free,
then $79/month
billed quarterly)

The Hack: Ever wanted to reach through the screen, grab a customer by the shoulders and ask them why they're not making a purchase? While we can't help you defy the laws of physics, nor break the space-time continuum, we can show you how to create quick and easy exit questions to get instant visitor feedback.

Your website is your most important digital marketing tool, and your website visitors provide your biggest opportunity to monetize this channel. Traditionally, it's been impossible to query your visitors "in the heat of the moment" while they're browsing your site, deciding whether to purchase or click the back button and head to your competitor's site.

Qualaroo was launched by Sean Ellis (typically regarded as the Godfather of Growth Hacking) and allows you to ask your visitors questions as they navigate through your site. This allows you the marketer to better understand their needs and their challenges, and ensures your site is meeting them. Qualaroo lets you deploy mini-surveys or questions based on the visitor's navigation and based on their previous answers.

Now Hack It:

- Sign up for a small business account at Qualaroo.com.

- Install the JavaScript snippet on your site.This only needs to be done once, and Qualaroo has easy to follow instructions.

- Create and design your first pop up survey.

- Target your survey to determine where and when it will appear.

- Log in to your dashboard to view results and reporting.

PRO TIP:
You can also question visitors who purchased a product, to find out what attracted them to the product and what (if anything) almost stopped them from making a purchase.

13

THE HEAT MAP HACK

How to collect data about customer website activity (so you can make your product better)

THE PHASE:
Pre Launch -
On-going

DIFFICULTY:
Intermediate

WE USE:
Trialfire.com
(Free plans for
start-ups)

The Hack: If hearing the words "data collection" makes you imagine hacking into the Matrix, we're here to prove just how easy it's gotten over the years. This hack will show you how to achieve things previously reserved for only those with technical coding skills. Through this hack you'll be able to track how people use your website or application, and use that data to unlock deep insights that help you grow your business, all without needing an engineering - or data-scientist - degree.

Now Hack It:

- Sign up for a free account attrialfire.com

- Add their code snippet to your site.

- Trialfire will automatically begin collecting every page-view, click, form submission and other action on your site.

- Build reports by clicking directly on your website, no frustrating report builders required.

- Create segments of your visitors in just a couple of clicks for use in targeted marketing campaigns.

PRO TIP:
Use their one-click integrations to sync data with your e-commerce, marketing or CRM software.

14

THE NICK EUBANKS HACK

How to hack the best keyword research for SEO and SEM

THE PHASE:
Pre Launch

DIFFICULTY:
Expert

WE USE:
TermExlorer.com
(FREE accounts
available but their
$97/year plan
is required for
advanced uses)

UberSuggest.org

adwords.google.
com/Keyword-
Planner

The Hack: Buzzwords are like pop songs, you hear a new one each week. You get tired of everyone talking endlessly about it. And just when you're ready to club the next person who mentions it, a new one comes along. But good ideas are like rock anthems. They're good no matter how many times you've heard it and they tend to stick around for a long time.

SEO, Pay Per Click, Blogging and Content Marketing are just few such "anthems" that aren't going anywhere. At the root of all these important marketing levers is keyword research. Knowing which keywords to target and promote can be the difference between life and death for a start-up. So pay attention kids.

Keywords are the key to much of your online marketing, so give them the attention they deserve. Google's keyword planner tool is a good place to start, but many services exist to take their base list and turn them into a huge list.

Once you start spending money on AdWords, you'll quickly learn which keywords are the most profitable and then focus your resources on those ones. Until then, you want to cast a huge net, because you never know which keywords will be the prize catch.

Now Hack It:

- Start with good old Google Keyword Planner. Search for new keywords by entering the top "head" keyword for your industry. Make sure country and language are set correctly.

- Click "get ideas" and then toggle over to "keywords" to view the results. Export them to a CSV file.

- Head over to UberSuggest.org and type your head keyword into their tool. They'll go letter by letter and expand your list dramatically. Add and export all those keywords to your list.

- Next we'll use a very powerful tool called Term Explorer. Term Explorer will take your huge list and populate it with competitive search data and SEOdata, which will become your master keyword list.

- Start a "bulk keyword job" by uploading your keyword list.

- When it finishes, select all keywords and send them for analysis. This will populate the keywords with the data.

PRO TIP:
Nick Eubanks has produced an unbelievable blog post on keyword research that walks you through the entire process. Read it at
http://www.seonick.net/keyword-research/

15

THE RESPONSIVE FORM HACK

How to create an awesome form based website

THE PHASE:
Pre Launch

DIFFICULTY:
Intermediate

WE USE:
Typeform.com
(FREE for basic,
$20/month
for Pro)

The Hack: Want a highly interactive landing page that contains a form or survey interface that converts higher than a typical customer survey? You'll be amazed at the data you can gather when you offer a beautiful user experience. Buy a domain, mask the forward and Bob's your uncle.

Remember when we spoke earlier of a hack that can take your MVP (Minimal Viable Product) and make it look bigger and better? Well, we love ideas like that so much, we have one more. With Typeform, you can create a super slick looking Web Form and embed it onto a website, creating a lead generating landing page that looks great and is fun for the user.

With a huge suite of integrations, you can also connect your form to a ton of different services, so if you want the email addresses to land in your MailChimp lists, it's easy to do.

Sometimes a little bit of design can go a long, long way, and that's exactly we love Typeform. We think you will too! These forms will even look great on mobile.

Now Hack It:

- Head over toTypeform.com and create a free account.

- Just like with the Survey Monkey hack, use their form creator to create a good looking form, either starting with a template or starting from scratch. Pay special attention to the customization options, because you want this form to look great, and you want the "introduction" page to compel people to fill out the form.

- Use the "configure" tab to customize your form by adding a progress bar, customizing the thank you email and determining where the results get forwarded to. You can also integrate any third party services here, such as MailChimp or Sales Force.

- Finally on the "distribute" tab, select and copy the URL link. Then head over to your domain registrar, buy the domain of your choice, and forward the domain (with masking) to the Typeform URL for your form. Now visitors will see your introduction page and will be prompted to fill out your form.

PRO TIP:
Once you get comfortable with Typeform, use their conditional logic to ask respondents different questions, based on how they answered the previous question.

16

THE LEAD SCORING HACK

How to automate lead scoring to funnel leads to specific pages

THE PHASE:
Pre Launch

DIFFICULTY:
Advanced

WE USE:
Typeform.com
($20/month Pro
package required
for this hack)

The Hack: Imagine a web form that could be the "Inspector Gadget" of web forms. One that could collect lead data, score each lead and direct them to a specific landing page, based on their score. Sounds impossible? Expensive? Well we're here to tell you that none of the above are needed. Here's why:

We had a client who wanted their visitors to submit a lead form, which would score them based on their answers, and send them to one of three different landing pages, depending on their score. Typically, this would be a custom (expensive) project, but we put our growth hacking hats on and figured out how to use Formstack to solve this problem.

The secret involved learning how to score the key questions and then having a hidden field for the total score (which the user didn't see). Based on that total score, the user got one of three confirmation messages and calls to action.

Now Hack It:

- Create a free account at Formstack.com

- You should now be getting the hang of creating forms using the various visual editors. Do the same with your lead form.

- Scoring questions: These four types of questions can be scored - select list, checkbox, number and radio buttons. Once your question is entered, select "advanced options editor" and values to each answer. These are the scores for each answer.

- Total lead scoring: Create a number field question, and make it "hidden." Define the value as the sum of the scored questions. So if you have four scored questions, have this value equal the sum of all four responses. Make sure it's hidden; you don't want leads seeing it.

- Routing logic: Once your form is complete, go to Settings -> Emails & Redirects -> After the Form is Submitted. Set the routing logic for each of the three grade score ranges, based on the hidden total score answer.

- Custom Message: For each score range, you can redirect to an external landing page or you can display a custom message. If the latter, make sure to set up a custom message for each of the three rules you created above.

- Now each lead gets sent the appropriate messaging, based on how they're scored.

PRO TIP:
Use custom messages for short and simple calls to action. Use external landing pages for more detailed offerings.

CASE STUDY #2
ROB WALLING
CO-FOUNDER, DRIP

Solving for Product-Market Fit

Drip was founded in late 2012 with the mutual frustration of Rob Walling and Derrick Reimer with the current email marketing and marketing apps on the market. Rob's aim for Drip was to give people power without being overly complicated, an aim that had still eluded marketing software.

Drip is lightweight marketing automation that doesn't suck. It allows customers to "craft every interaction with your leads, trial users and customers like an artisan." What makes Drip so unique is it's simple to use yet very powerful. Using Drip you can trigger an email, campaign or tag based on any action a user takes, be it expressing interest in a topic, downloading an ebook, or starting a trial.

Today, Drip is one of the best email marketing apps, however its journey to achieve this success was far from simple. According to Co-Founder Rob Walling, Drip's first traction goal was to obtain $20 thousand dollars per month of recurring revenue within six months after launching. This meant acquiring approximately 300 customers. Unfortunately, six months after the launch Drip had only managed to earn between eight and ten thousand dollars per month, well below the initial target.

Analyzing the data, Rob identified a very specific reason for failing to meet the target... product-market fit. "We didn't have a product that people would stick around and use. I was driving tons of traffic, and lots of people would sign-up and start trials, and then they would just churn out." Churn rate is the amount of customers or subscribers who discontinue with your service or company during a given time period. When you only have 100 - 200 customers, you cannot get an accurate cohort churn, so instead Rob calculated the simple churn which he describes as "the total number that canceled divided by the number of customers.". For Drip it's simple churn was over 20 per cent, meaning it was losing almost a fifth of its customers every month. Ideally Rob wanted to see that number well below 10 percent.

At this stage Rob knew that without solving the retention problem, any marketing efforts would be futile. Rob and his co-founder Derrick spent the next 60 days figuring out why the churn was so high, and the following five weeks building the solution to that question. In the end Rob describes it as a pivot from email marketing to marketing automation.

It was clear to the Drip team that in order to achieve $20 thousand in monthly recurring revenue, product-market fit would have to be met. Here is how Drip achieved product-market fit and achieved its traction goals:

Adjust for Product-Market Fit

No product or service survives first contact with customers. The best way to begin adjusting for product-market fit is by conducting customer interviews. For Rob this meant adopting a "constant contact" approach by calling and emailing everyone who used Drip to gain feedback. Drip received very useful feedback from early adopters who had skin in the game. These were people who had been following Drip and had signed up for the early launch list. During this process a number of themes appeared. For Drip one such theme was people loved the app, the UI and UX, but it was too expensive for what it does. This became an important theme, rather than drop the price they asked themselves, "what value do we provide that will make people say, oh crap, this is cheap!". This distinction led Drip to focus on developing marketing automation tools, which at the time were very expensive and complex. As the Drip team slowly added marketing automation tools, they noticed that trails decreased and the monthly recurring revenue started increasing. Once the team started to find product-market fit, they noticed the churn plummeted by almost half from around 20 percent to 10 percent.

Build a Brand that Resonates with your customers

Companies can over complicate growth when many times the simplest changes can yield the biggest improvements. For Drip it was not enough to just build new features into its product, it had to reposition its brand to resonate with current and potential customers. One of Rob's founder friends suggested a new headline "Lightweight Marketing Automation that doesn't suck.". They tested this headline over a two month period while batting around other concepts like "we help you send emails to your trial users and customers based on their behavior.". Rob describes the main problem with the second headline "it's too long and cumbersome, it's trying to describe what you do instead of what you are." Once Drip repositioned their brand they could effectively target and attract users who are in need of their solution to marketing automation.

Create Mystery in Pre-Launch or Build a pre-launch list

Many first time entrepreneurs overlook the importance of building a pre-launch list. For Rob this was an important focus that would ensure they would have paying customers from day one of launch. Rob's pre-launch strategy which he calls "concentric-circle marketing" was very effective at acquiring pre-signups. Rob used a variety of channels from his personal network to podcasts, blogging, online PR and Facebook ads to build a pre-launch list of approximately 3,400 people. With concentric-circle marketing you start with the innermost circle which is your direct audience. For Rob these were people who listened to his podcast and read his blog. Using his inner circle he was able to acquire around 500 to 1,000 signups.

The second circle out is your friends and colleagues. In Rob's case this meant a mini press tour within his network, from appearing on podcasts to being featured on popular blogs. These channels drove approximately 1,000 to 1,500 signups.

The final circle is what Rob calls a "cold audience", people that he did not know. What worked for him was targeting marketers using facebook ads and driving them to his landing page. Using this channel he spent about $3.50 per ad and acquired approximately 1,000 signups.

When we asked Rob what the biggest insights he learned that would help fellow entrepreneurs and marketers he said:

First, "Let influencers in early and knock their socks off." Involving influencers early does two things: first, it leverages their feedback and second it builds a sense of ownership turning them into champions of your startup. These people have their own audiences and will be motivated to share your company. This can be a very effective way of growing your pre-launch list and getting early users.

Secondly, "You only get to launch once." Don't launch early and ship or release a bad product. This insight is counter-intuitive to the majority of startup advice which is launch early and fail fast. While this advice has its benefits it can also be very catastrophic if your product does not retain. You typically only get one crack at a customer so if you release a bad product to your entire audience you potentially can bleed all the good prospects out and months of hard work.

Finally, "Be wary of advice from free users." When taking feedback from users Rob highlighted how important it was to have customers that he knew and trusted. As you conduct customer interviews it's critical to be able to separate good feedback from bad. With free users it's hard to tell who is serious about your product and who is just giving feedback. The problem with taking advice from free users is that people who are not paying and may never pay are influencing product decisions. When you have users that you know and trust using your product/service their advice will land with much more credence and credibility.

17

THE PHONE-A-FRIEND HACK

How to get the perfect advice you need without having a huge network

THE PHASE:
Pre Launch

DIFFICULTY:
Easy

WE USE:
Clarity.fm (per minute advice calls)

Inbound.org (free engaged forum)

Guides.co (free guides and paid guides)

The Hack: What the best part about being Mark Zuckerberg? Ok, aside from the speedboats and designer hoodies? That's right, it's his network. If Mark is having a problem, he can grab the phone and call any CEO to solicit their experiences. Unfortunately, you can't. But try some of these hacks to get the advice you need, on demand.

As an entrepreneur, having an amazing network is worth its weight in gold. However, it's quite hard to hack a network - a trusted network requires many years of investment into relationships, giving without taking and adding value to their lives. It's not something that can be done in a pinch.

However, there are a number of sites and services we use all the time to get the right advice, from people who have the right experiences, at just the right time. With a little bit of research and a touch of effort, you can get Yoda level advice on the challenges you're facing, and use that advice to make the best decisions. As Yoda would say, "Powerful that is."

Now Hack It:

- As with any of these sites and services, a little bit of preparation goes a long way. Familiarize yourself with the sites and establish a presence before asking for advice.

- Clarity.fm is our favorite for getting TOP quality advice quickly and efficiently. They have over 10,000 experts of all types (categorized and tagged very specifically), who make themselves available on a per minute fee, to dispense advice and point you in the right direction.

- Search profiles until you find the perfect expert and book a time with them. Be prepared so your call is as efficient as possible.

- Inbound.org is a community for people interested in inbound marketing. With over 30,000 engaged members, you can become knowledgeable very quickly just by following the trending discussions. Once you get the hang of it, participate in community discussions and post your own questions.

- Guides.co is a collection of resources to help you with a specific objective, such as "Get More PR for your Start-up". Their guides are like checklists on steroids, and have the instructions and templates needed to achieve the goal.

- As an example, our co-author Jeff has a guide called "Brand Partnerships," teaching how to negotiate deals with large companies when you have no leverage.

PRO TIP:
Don't balk at the per minute prices on Clarity.fm (well except for the crazy ones like Mark Cuban's $166.67/minute). Even rates as high as $10/minute over a 15 minute call can produce extraordinary results, making the $150 investment a no-brainer.

18

THE BLOG HACK

How to start a blog in under 5 minutes

THE PHASE:
Pre Launch

DIFFICULTY:
Easy

WE USE:
Wordpress.com
(FREE)

Bluehost.com
($3.95/month
hosting)

The Hack: When's the best time to launch a blog? 18 months ago. When's the next best time? Today! It's easy to do, it engages your brand with your customers and it provides free organic traffic for years! The updated content on your site also signals to Google that you have a hand on the tiller. Ahoy!

When we talk about content marketing, a lot of times that simply involves creating amazing content through a blog, and then amplifying its reach through social media, email and paid channels. Sounds a lot easier than content marketing, doesn't it?

Starting a blog has all kinds of benefits, depending on your objectives. Blogging can position you as a thought leader, can generate organic traffic through search, and can generate valuable inbound links that help with SEO. Think of every blog post as the answer to a question that your customers search frequently.

With a bit of effort, your blog post on a specific topic can be the top search result for that customer search query. And that means organic traffic for months or years to come. Creating an organic traffic stream based on evergreen content is one of the few remaining marketing channels where you can gain leverage.

Now Hack It:

- Select one of the many web hosts that offer one click WordPress installation. BlueHost and Go Daddy are both popular choices.

- Buying your domain name from the same company that hosts your site will avoid having to transfer the domain between hosting companies. Consider several different popular domain extensions (i.e. .com, .net) when choosing the perfect domain.

- Every blog needs to run blogging software and WordPress is the most popular choice, powering over 19% of the world's websites! Use the one-click install functionality to install it quickly and easily.

- Wordpress has a ton of amazing themes to choose from, so you don't have to design your blog from scratch. Install one of the many free themes, or search themeforest.net for paid theme options.

- Login to your blog dashboard and start blogging. Develop a blogging theme within which you'll select weekly topics. Some people prefer writing several at a time, and then scheduling their releases in advance. Think quality over quantity and vary the medium when you can (text posts, video posts, graphical posts etc).

PRO TIP:
Make sure that your blog posts are incorporating your most important keywords.

19

THE PRE-TARGETING HACK

How to warm up your audience before advertising to them

THE PHASE:
Pre Launch

DIFFICULTY:
Intermediate

WE USE:
Facebook or
AdWords

The Hack: You have that nice long list of emails opt-in emails that you want to utilize for your growth hacking purposes. The email list may not even be an opt-in one and but we're certainly not here to judge… The point is that you want the emails sent to that list to have as high of an engagement rate as possible. Easier said than done, especially if the list wasn't organically grown in the first place. But there is a way to get yourself in the good books - or, in this case, inboxes - of your future email recipients. It involves what is known as email "pre-targeting." If you know what retargeting is then this is essentially the opposite of that.

But retargeting is retroactive whereas growth hacking is all about embracing the future. So is pre-targeting, which works by allowing you to get your branded ads in front of the email list before they receive the first piece of communication from you. This makes the ensuing email a lot less "cold" and should increase your open rates.

Now Hack It:

- There are a number of online ad platforms available for you to carry out your pre-targeting campaigns on: Facebook, Twitter, Gmail, Google Adwords and others.

- They all have their own name for their retargeting service but the logic is similar - you upload a list of email addresses and ads are then served targeting those specific individuals:

- Facebook calls it "Custom Audiences"

- Twitter calls it "Tailored Audiences"

- Upload your email list following the instructions on Facebook or Twitter.

- Don't worry about having a CTA as the goal is to create familiarity with your brand. You're "warming up" the list, remember?

- Once you've successfully finished your campaign, then your subsequent email blast will be less likely to fall on deaf ears.

- Sit back and enjoy the higher open and click-through rates. You've deserved them!

20
THE LIST
BUILDER HACK

How to start building up your email list

THE PHASE:
Pre Launch

DIFFICULTY:
Intermediate

WE USE:
MailChimp.com
(FREE up to
12,000 monthly
emails and 2000
subscribers)

The Hack: Alright, no smiling now. Time to get serious. We're about to discuss the highest converting channel out there - email marketing. One of your top priorities during pre-launch is to collect as many qualified email addresses as you can. With a healthy email list you can market to a pre-engaged customer based and you can create massive, custom audiences based on the characteristics of your list. Now that's some growth hacking Ninja stuff.

Even though dozens of marketing trends have come and gone, email marketing has continued to remain one of the highest converting channels in the marketing tool kit. That's why it's really important to have a lead generating website that reliably contributes email addresses into the top of your marketing funnel. Once inside the funnel, we can use drip campaigns to nurture the leads throughout the buying process.

With this in mind, it's important for B2C companies to think like lead generators, with every email addresses being a lead and every lead being nurtured. Combining a lead generating landing page with an email marketing platform such as MailChimp creates a powerful pre-launch campaign. It makes sense too, because your most valuable leads are those that sign-up for early access.

Now Hack It:

- Head over to MailChimp.com and create a free account. Your account will remain free until you surpass 2,000 subscribers, at which point you'll be asked to upgrade.

- Once in MailChimp, create lists for each of your target market segments. If you only have one email input form, or you're not segmenting your list yet, just create one list.

- Use the industry preferred double opt-in process, so the list is clean and there's never any doubt as to your customer's permission.

- Integrate your MailChimp list with your landing page, so that the email addresses get stored directly into MailChimp. To do so, you'll need your MailChimp API key (don't freak out, this is simple).Go to Account -> Extras -> API keys and Create a Key. Enter this key into your landing page dashboard such as Unbounce.com

- If your landing page doesn't integrate with MailChimp you have two easy options: create a Zap at zapier.com or export the email addresses from the landing page and import them into MailChimp.

PRO TIP:
Sometimes it's better to give than to receive. Think of a downloadable piece of content that your customers would love. Offer them this content in exchange for their email address. You'll collect more emails and your customers will feel good about you, wanting to return the favor.

21

THE BULLSEYE HACK

How to hack a launch marketing plan

THE PHASE:
Pre Launch

DIFFICULTY:
Intermediate

WE USE:
TractionBook.com
(FREE resources
available, but take
our word and buy
the book!)

The Hack: One of our favorite marketing books of all time is called "Traction," written by Gabriel Weinberg and Justin Mares. In their book, they introduce a methodology called Bullseye, which brainstorms, analyzes and ranks marketing concepts over 19 different proven marketing channels.

The result - you'll select three channels to test cheaply and in parallel, with hopes of finding a promising channel to scale and optimize. This is the real deal folks, try it out.

The reason we love this book is that the Bullseye methodology is designed to overcome what the authors call "founder biases" which biases marketers towards or away from certain channels, based on past business and personal experience. Bullseye forces marketers to consider all channels and brainstorm ideas they never would have.

By the time you've gone through the exercise, you will have a detailed launch/traction marketing plan to test three channels, including experiments you'll run to quantify the channels.

Now Hack It:

- Grab a copy of the book "Traction" by Weinberg and Mares.

- Quickly read the first five chapters as it walks you through the process. The rest of the chapters focus on each of the 19 marketing channels.

- Get your entire team involved in the bullseye process as they likely have many interesting ideas.

- Once you've brainstormed all 19 channels, you need to rank them into three categories: the outer circle (unlikely to succeed), the middle circle (possibilities) and the inner circle (the ideas you like the best).

- Make sure you have no more or less than three inner circle channels to test.

- Design small tests to evaluate each of the chosen three channels. Remember, you're not looking for ROI off the bat; rather you're looking for a "sign of life" that the channel might be valuable.

- Hopefully you'll find a channel that shows some promise, and you'll begin to optimize, scale and test further. If you didn't, go back to the "middle circle" and test three more. page dashboard such as Unbounce.com

PRO TIP:
One of the key take-away from "Traction" is an "a-ha" moment for many marketers: Companies only need ONE profitable channel to be wildly successful. You don't need to be successful in all the channels.

CASE STUDY #3
AARON
HOUGHTON
CO-FOUNDER
AND CEO,
BOOST SUITE

Market Early, Market Often

BoostSuite is a web marketing automation product for small businesses. In just five minutes you can setup an account to boost your content, audience and business. Where other web marketing automation products tend to be complex and difficult to use, BoostSuite empowers novice web marketers to grow website traffic and convert more online visitors into customers and leads for their business.

Back in 2012, BoostSuite was an early stage software startup with only 50 alpha users. Before a product gets to see the light of day and begin beta testing with "real users", it must pass alpha testing, generally done by employees of the company. At this time, BoostSuite was an on-page search engine optimization tool targeted at small business marketers. On-page optimization refers to the actual HTML code, meta tags, keyword placements and keyword density of your website.

The early product helped marketers attract more website visitors from search engines, and convert those visitors into customers. One of the clever tools that BoostSuite offered during the app's onboarding process for new users was a letter grade based on their website's current level of optimization.

According to Aaron Houghton, co-founder and CEO, his goal was, "to acquire as many small businesses as possible for the beta version of our free plan, so that we can entice them to upgrade to one of our paid tiers." In order to achieve this goal, several different user acquisition experiments were tested to acquire beta users. By the end of the beta period, Aaron wanted to have real results to determine which channels were most effective.

With a clear strategy in mind, here is how BoostSuite acquired its beta users:

Pre-Launch Promotion with LaunchRock

Companies need to be able to sell vaporware when they don't have a finished product. To start acquiring users for the beta version, Aaron created a simple landing page using LaunchRock. The landing page allows visitors to sign up and promote your business to unlock early access to the products or services you will eventually launch. To entice people to refer friends, extra visitor capacity was offered on BoostSuite's top free plan.If a user has more than 3,000 monthly pageviews, they would be required to pay $19/month to continue. The LaunchRock promotion would increase the per month pageviews limit to 5,000 indefinitely. In order to promote the campaign, the BoostSuite team sent an email urging their friends to help find new users. The email contained a link to the landing page on LaunchRock and explained the referral promotion and rewards. At the end of the 30 day campaign, 455 users were acquired with 11.9 per cent of those referred by users on the initial announcement email. The full cost of the LaunchRock campaign, including the team's time, was approximately $150, the cost per free account created was only 33 cents.

Test multiple messages with Google Adwords

The importance of getting your messaging right has been a common theme. Don't make the mistake of assuming you know what people want to hear. One of the best ways to do this is through A/B testing your messaging to see what people actually respond to. One of the channels that Aaron experimented with was searching text ads with Google Adwords. Several different messaging strategies were tested to determine which were the most effective at getting people to click and visit the website. Headlines and general text like "get more website traffic", "increase search engine ranking", "get your website grade", and "how does your website score?" were tested. What Aaron found was the text ads that mentioned the website grade performed the best, with click through rates as high as 6.22 per cent. Using this tactic, Aaron now had real data to determine how to most effectively reach potential customers.

Bigcommerce App Marketplace Integration

Focusing on existing platforms that already have an established and massive user base can be a very effective tactic. For Aaron, Bigcommerce, an app marketplace was the perfect fit for his SEO optimization solution. Users find apps through the default "featured apps" screen and through categories like "marketing", where BoostSuite was featured for a limited time. Once the featured period had expired, apps were ranked solely by the average star rating. To effectively optimize the Bigcommerce platform, Aaron made sure to provide exceptional service to all Bigcommerce users, with welcome phone calls, dedicated assistance with account setup and priority email ticket handling. Through these efforts, BoostSuite earned 17 five star ratings from customers, keeping the app listing near the top of the marketing apps category for many months. Although these efforts required intensive software development and customer service support, costing roughly $5,500, it did produce 495 free accounts created during the year, giving a cost of $11.11 per free account.

Through these campaigns, BoostSuite acquired nearly 4,000 small business users for its beta and early launch periods. The real benefit however, was in the thousands of questions and recommendations that were provided, allowing the team to further refine the offering. In fact, many of these early beta testers converted into monthly paid subscribers. In Aaron's own words, "the campaigns were a huge success and exceeded our goals." However, Aaron was quick to point out that comparing the results of each tactic to one another would be misleading. Each tactic had its own tangible cost per free account but, "because each tactic had investment periods and return periods of different lengths and their own maximum scale, they can't be evaluated only by that number." For example, even though the LaunchRock campaign provided the lowest cost per free account, it also had limited scale. Google Adwords on the other hand has a huge ability to scale, but with a budget of only $3,419, it only purchased a small share of the total search traffic for the best performing terms. In Aaron's mind, "despite having a cost per free account three times higher than LaunchRock, Google Adwords would be a logical tactic to turn to for further user acquisition." Finally, when looking at the Bigcommerce tactic, although it had huge upfront costs, it required almost zero development cost to keep it going.

So what did Aaron feel marketers should take away from his experience?

First, try everything. To achieve the pre-launch goals, Aaron and his team tried many other experiments and promotional tactics to drive early users, some worked but many didn't. Don't assume you know which channels will convert the best, try as many as possible and use data to drive decisions.

Second, test small. In Aaron's own words, "spend as little as possible." Start by prioritizing the tests which let you measure early results as soon as possible. Run a simple experiment with a small investment, around $200-$500 to determine if that channel will be worth continuing to use.

Finally, find partners. Start by targeting partners who are already working with your target customers. As Aaron did with Bigcommerce, "start first with partners that have open API's and will let you reach their customers through a marketplace or other automated means of promotion."

SECTION 02

TRANSITION TO GROWTH

Once you have proof that you've achieved Product/Market Fit, it's time to light up the second-stage rocket boosters and start searching for growth. In this stage your going to be more scientist than marketer, so make sure your data skills are sharp and you're measuring the right metrics, usually customer acquisition cost.

At this point, you really want to get away from a campaign-based approach to marketing and start thinking about building 'marketing machines' that provide scalable, predictable, dependable revenue. A good growth marketer approaches this phase with an open mind and a healthy curiosity to experiment with different channels, different marketing opportunities and different funnels.

Using Traction's Bullseye Methodology, you can analyze and identify testable opportunities to "poke the box" and measure the results. At this point of trial and error, you're not searching for perfection but more for signs of life that the channel may be successful, if optimized in the future.

Take all your customer development research and refine your unique value proposition to highlight the benefits that your early customers liked the most. Establish a lifetime value hypothesis for how much a customer is worth to your company. You can use this metric to estimate how much you can afford to spend to acquire the customer. Ensure that your systems are scalable, so that as you grow, your people and your technology can handle a rapid influx of customers. Oftentimes, early startups don't prepare for the customer service demands that arise with rapid growth. This is truly important because fixing a problem identified through customer support is MUCH cheaper than alternative acquisition tactics.

In Tomasz Tunguz's post "Milestones to Startup Success", he offers up some milestones that startups can look towards as inflection points to adapt their acquisition strategy. He suggests focusing on "brand experience" over "brand awareness" and creating an experience that is remarkable and shareable: "It is much cheaper and more effective for startups to focus on creating a fantastic brand experience".

Marketing ROI begins to play a larger role, because you are searching for channels that have the promise to scale cost effectively and maintain the unit economics of the early test results. However, it's still not the most phase appropriate factor for this transitional stage, or as Tunguz puts it "While ROI lets you know if a user acquisition channel is sustainable, the key focus should be on exposing lots of the right people to your fantastic product experience".

What separates growth marketers from traditional marketers is an insatiable curiosity about testing new channels, measuring their effectiveness and scaling the channels that work. Many traditional marketers focus on scaling channels BEFORE they know they'll work, and end up wasting a lot of time and money in the process.

Growth marketers can begin to move off of expensive direct response channels and focus higher in the funnel, where educational and content initiatives become more valuable. Thinking about the channels as a funnel, focusing on driving more good leads and nurturing customers over a longer sales cycle allows you to scale in channels that promise to be more proprietary and less competitive.

The key here is to approach growth marketing with an open mind, try out a lot of different tactics, but only focus, optimize and scale once you've seen a sign of life.

Now let's light up those second stage booster and get to growing!

22

THE WAITLIST HACK

How to create a viral pre-launch signup form

THE PHASE:
Launch

DIFFICULTY:
Intermediate

WE USE:
Kickoff Labs or
Viral Signups

The Hack: Why acquire only one user at a time when you can get two, three, four or even more in one fell swoop? While this may sound like a utopian pre-launch dream, it is a possibility if you just implement this one little hack. Sure, you may already have a landing page for your app that allows people to leave their email and join your "waiting list" but, often, that's where the buck stops. However, you want your buck to keep on buckin' until the Twitterverse is awash with mentions of your digital creation. The solution is to provide your users with a viral sign-up form. Those who share your app with x-number of their friends get to go on your launch list. Those who share more get to move higher up the wait list. Simple, right? But you just wait until this hack is live!

Now Hack It:

- This is how the process works:
- Your future "waitlister" signs up using an email opt-in form.
- After signing up, they receive a custom URL that can be shared with their friends.
- The URL is trackable and you set up an email auto-responder series to send emails notifying the waitlister every time someone has signed up as a result of their invites andadvising them that they are now officially on your launch list.
- Once they have invited the required number of people, they get a final email.
- Of course you could code this all up yourself or but why reinvent the wheel? Here are some Wordpress plugins that will help you to implement this system quickly and easily:
- Viral Sign-ups - this one is free for up to 10,000 subscribers
- KickoffLabs' Viral Signup Form Plugin - plans start at $29 per month

23
THE UPVOTE
HACK

How to make sharing easier with an upvote website widget

THE PHASE:
Launch

DIFFICULTY:
Easy

WE USE:
Love It Pro

The Hack: Why acquire only one user at a time when you can get two, three, four or even more in one fell swoop? While this may sound like a utopian pre-launch dream, it is a possibility if you just implement this one little hack. Sure, you may already have a landing page for your app that allows people to leave their email and join your "waiting list" but, often, that's where the buck stops. However, you want

your buck to keep on buckin' until the Twitterverse is awash with mentions of your digital creation. The solution is to provide your users with a viral sign-up form. Those who share your app with x-number of their friends get to go on your launch list. Those who share more get to move higher up the wait list. Simple, right? But you just wait until this hack is live!

Just Hack It:

- What do people really, REALLY like doing on sites such as Buzzfeed or Reddit?

- No, not looking at LOLcat photos….

- No, not creating useless listicles on every conceivable topic…

- Here it is: they like having a direct say in what content becomes popular and what content gets relegated to the bottom of the virtual junk heap.

- Users of such sites like to be HEARD. They do so by promoting the content that catches their fancy...

- Even if the only thing they choose to have a say in is upvoting the thousands LOLcat memes they've seen that month.

- And that's our keyword: upvoting. It can do wonders for your blog's metrics.

- The Love It Pro Wordpress plugin puts this upvoting power in your reader's hands without the hassle of having to implement a full-blown gamification framework.

- Now your readers can upvote the content that they like most and, in return, feel more invested in your blog's success.

- In return, you feel good because you know that someone, somewhere, kind-of cares. Kind-of…

- Getting kudos has never been so easy!

24

THE INVITE-A-FRIEND HACK

How to create a viral invite a friend "thank you" page

THE PHASE:
Launch

DIFFICULTY:
Intermediate

WE USE:
Lead Pages

The Hack: Consider this scenario. You've just opted into a new email subscription. Most likely, you ended up on a "thank you" page that said something along the lines of: "Thank you for subscribing. You'll soon get a bland email from us asking you to confirm your subscription. Please, pretty please don't accidentally delete it and, just in case, check your spam folder." Seems a pretty logical confirmation page to show your new subscriber, right? Wrong! Think about it. Your visitor was impressed enough by your content to subscribe to your newsletter. Out of the hundreds of millions that are out there. At that precise moment in time, they're in the most compliant state that you're likely to find them. You definitely DON'T want to then show a generic "Thank you… blah blah blah" page. Read below to learn how to seize such golden opportunities.

Just Hack It:

- What you need to do now is capitalize on your new subscriber's euphoric state and hit them with a confirmation page that asks them to do something.

- That "something" can be telling their friends about your product or getting them to sign-up to your webinar. Whatever it is that you ask for, the goal is to strike while the iron's hot!

- The landing page needs to be simple and hyper-focused on your CTA.

- There's not much more to it than that. This really is a simple hack that will help to channel your subscriber's positive feelings into increased word-of-mouth for your start-up.

- By the way, if you use their landing page app, LeadPages offer a free page template to

- save you having to develop one from scratch.

25

THE PRESS HACK

How to use the power of the crowd to create a press list

THE PHASE:
Launch

DIFFICULTY:
Advanced

WE USE:
Amazon
Mechanical Turk

The Hack: You know that you need publicity. The problem is that you're no PR extraordinaire and, most likely, neither are your co-founders. But you do want the glory of being featured on the front page of TechCrunch or TheNextWeb. Boy, do you want the glory! Sorry, but so does every other SaaS founder on the planet. This hack is meant to provide a way for you to target your publicity efforts so that you get the most bang for your buck and substantially increase your press coverage.

Just Hack It:

- Scour Google News for reporters who have already covered apps similar to yours. If your app is SO "stealth mode" or "uniquely out-of-this-world" then seek reporters who may have experience in your industry

- Use http://press.customerdevlabs.com/to turn your search results into a convenient spreadsheet (yes, there's an app for that!)

- Upload your list to Mechanical Turk in order to automate the process of finding each reporter's contact details (you don't really want to sift through several hundred news listings, do you now?)

- Voila, you now have a list of reporters that is as long as your arm. Now is the time to polish off your press kit. Or start working on one...

- Make sure to embargo your press release but be aware that some large news websites can't stand this practice!

- Set-up alerts for web and social mentions using your favorite tools.

26

THE INFLUENCER HACK

How to target influencers using Followerwonk, Klout or Brand24

THE PHASE:
Launch

DIFFICULTY:
Intermediate

WE USE:
Followerwonk

The Hack: We are all drowning in a sea of information and the only way to keep our heads above the water is by filtering the noise. Most people, including your users, do this by finding individuals whom they consider to be influential in their chosen niches and then ignore most of the other noise. Such influencers become gatekeepers of relevant content and can become a growth hacker's best marketing allies. In fact, a well-timed cold email, Tweet or LinkedIn InMail message to the right influencer can catapult your app from relative obscurity straight into the SaaS big leagues. Reaching out to influencers, if done right, is one of the most effective ways of quickly hacking growth for your start-up. Which is all well and good, you say. But how do you find relevant influencers in your industry? How do you then ensure that they actually sit up and start paying attention to your product? Read below for solutions.

Just Hack It:

- The key to finding influencers is by using the multitude of tools that are available for this purpose.

- These person-to-person marketing tools consist of social media analytics and monitoring apps. They can be used to find out whom your users pay attention to and where relevant conversations are happening online.

- Some of the most popular apps for analyzing and growing your social graph include: Followerwonk, Topsy, Klout or Buzzsumo.

- You also need to monitor the conversations that your users are engaging in. Tools like Brand24, Mention and Talk Walker can all help you with this task.

- Now that know who your influencers are, it's time to take action! Mention them in your social conversations, reach out to them with cold or warm emails, connect with them on their chosen social networks, etc.

- Just get off your backside and start making it happen...

27

THE HARO
HACK

How to use Help A Reporter Out
to get you startup some PR

THE PHASE:
Launch

DIFFICULTY:
Easy

WE USE:
helpareporter.com
(FREE)

The Hack: A lot of PR generation involves pitching stories or "angles" to various journalists, hoping that your story catches their attention. Or you can provide them exactly what they're looking for, by monitoring your daily HARO (help a reporter) email. The email features a list of topics that journalists are looking for experts on. Find one that fits and pitch your story. If can bring the horse to water and all that!

Journalists use HARO to post their article topics in hopes of finding experts that can provide input and interviews for their piece. If you're lucky enough to find a topic that fits your company's story or expertise, you can reach out to the specific journalist and increase your odds of getting a valuable mention in their article or blog post.

Just Hack It:

- Head over to helpareporter.com and sign up for their daily digest email of reporter requests.

- Book time every day to quickly review the digests, looking for leads on reporter's articles that fit your stories.

- Reach out to the email address provided and pitch your story. Treat the pitch just like an outbound pitch and ensure that you're emphasizing the story ahead of your business.

- Wait for reporters to respond and schedule a time for an interview.

PRO TIP:
Set up a keyword filter in Gmail to search the HARO emails for keywords that match your company's stories and angles. That way, Google will flag the HARO emails that contain your keywords, and you can focus on those emails specifically.

28

THE SYNDICATION HACK

How to quickly syndicate your blog for additional inbound traffic

THE PHASE:
Launch

DIFFICULTY:
Intermediate

WE USE:
BoostSuite.
com (FREE for
1 article trade/
month, $19/
month for
unlimited
article trades)

The Hack: You've written the perfect blog post and it's up on your blog, but you haven't been visited by the "organic traffic fairy" yet. What can you do? Use BoostSuite, the co-marketing platform to trade content by having related sites post your blog post for new traffic.

BoostSuite.com offers what they call a co-marketing platform, which allows you to swap blog posts with other related but non-competitive websites. The result is that your blog post gets additional exposure, which can lead to new organic traffic sources and increased exposure for your blog. It also gives you additional content for your website that you would otherwise have to create.

Just Hack It:

- Visit BoostSuite.com and sign up for an account. If you plan on trading a lot of content, sign up for their $19/month plan, which gives you unlimited content trades. If you want to kick the tires first, their free account gives you one trade per month.

- Enter your competitor's websites for comparables.

- Upload any articles and blog posts you have written that you want to share.

- Add your most important keywords so the system knows what blog posts to recommend to you.

- Boost Suite will notify you when they have a content partner for you to trade with. You can review their posts and upload to your site.

PRO TIP:
Remember the best things come to those who wait, you don't need to jump at the first offer on the table if you're a little unsure about it.

29

THE SCIENTIFIC BLOGGING HACK

How to scrape your blog for clues on how to optimize it

THE PHASE:
Launch

DIFFICULTY:
Intermediate

WE USE:
Import.io and
Shared Count

The Hack: If you ever tried to improve your copywriting chops, then you may have come across a book called "Scientific Advertising" by Claude Hopkins. In his popular work, Mr. Hopkins lays out a framework for creating effective advertising. One of the most important points that he emphasizes is the need for copious amounts of testing and measuring. And as an A/B-wielding growth hacker you wholeheartedly agree, right? But this ain't the Summer of Love and blogs are one of the most effective "ads" online. So it's time to take your blogging and make it all scientific. But apart from analyzing the heck out of your posts with Google Analytics and running heat maps, what else can you do? Here's a hack that will help you to gain a better understanding of your blogging in order to improve the virality of your posts methodically. Just like a real growth scientist would.

Just Hack It:

- Download Import.io as this is the tool that you will use to scrape your blog.

- Create a crawler with Import.io and let it loose on your blog in order to extract everything, including meta-data.

- Export your data to Excel or Google Sheets.

- Now, go to SharedCount and upload your list of exported URLs - this will show you how much social love each post got.

- Now export the data from SharedCount and combine your blog meta and social sharing data using the VLOOKUP function.

- You can then play around with the data by combining various bits of meta information with the social data to see what insights you can gain.

- In addition to being a growth hacker, you are now officially a Blogging Growth Scientist.

30

THE TESTIMONIAL HACK

How to use customer testimonials to support each product feature

THE PHASE:
Launch

DIFFICULTY:
Easy

WE USE:
Nothing needed

The Hack: Credibility. It's what many new SaaS and tech start-ups struggle with and, some, sorely lack. And it's definitely not easy when apps disappear into the digital nothingness, often, without even so much as a sneak peak. Like wannabe actors who just can't beat their stage fright. There are also those start-ups that stick around for just long enough to burn through their Series A round but then turn into a black hole once the "fun money" dries up. Nothing more than a sad landing page with a one-sentence apology to show for the good times. While users are getting increasingly more tolerant of this general state of affairs, there's nothing like a good bit of old school social proof to make your start-up stand out. Here's an easy hack to help you to just that. Hint: it involves using testimonials...

Now Hack It:

- You're no doubt aware of best-practice guidelines that say to have user testimonials on your website to increase its perceived credibility.

- And no doubt, you've put up a couple of testimonials for good measure. Somewhere towards the end of your trendy parallax scroll one-page website. The very end.

- Here's a thought: why not add a customer testimonial under EACH feature that you shamelessly plug? This way, your testimonials are less generic and more believable. As every good copywriter knows, specifics sell!

- Hack over - get back to selling...

31

THE SKYSCRAPER HACK

How to use Buzzsumo to identify the most popular topics in your field

THE PHASE:
Launch

DIFFICULTY:
Intermediate

WE USE:
BuzzSumo

The Hack: Content marketing is hard work. There's a reason they call it "feeding the beast." And the more you feed it the hungrier it gets. It's easy to run out of content ideas and then think about running for the hills in order to get away from this content-crazy civilization of ours. But don't give up yet! There is an easier way to do this. Think about the number of blog posts and articles that you've seen after reading which you've thought to yourself: "I could expand on that and make it my own." Well, that is our Growth Hack of the Day for you. Here's a more detailed explanation of what you need to do.

Now Hack It:

- Do some sleuthing for content that ranks highly or is fairly visible in your industry. You can do this using apps such as BuzzSumo, Topsy and others.

- Take your newfound content, analyze it and then graft your own brilliant thoughts and ideas on top of it.

- Package your thoughts into a brand-spanking new blog post and reach out to the same people who promoted the original piece of content.

- There, no more searching in the abyss with a flashlight for content inspiration! It is now at your beck and call.

32

THE PRODUCT HUNT HACK

How to use Linkydink to create easy customer newsletter full of curated links

THE PHASE:
Launch

DIFFICULTY:
Intermediate

WE USE:
Linkydink

The Hack: Email is still the killer app, especially when it comes to converting users into paying customers. However, putting together a full-blown email marketing strategy takes time and a lot of effort to properly execute. Especially when your start-up is in its infancy, free time is a luxury and there may more urgent growth opportunities that you need to first pursue. So, how do you solve the dilemma of regularly showing up in your user's inboxes without having to commit a hefty amount of time to creating a full-blown email strategy? Read on to discover an app that can save your bacon and keep the MailChimp monkey off your back. For now.

Now Hack It:

- The answer to your email marketing allergy is link curation and it is the growth hack that helped launch ProductHunt.

- To make use of this awesome hack, register for an account at Linkydink. It will only cost $5 to expand your group beyond 5 subscribers. A fair price to pay for what will expand your acquisition channels with minimal time investment.

- Now you can start subscribing users left and right to your curated "link blasts" without having to worry about setting up auto-responders, drip campaigns and other such nonsense (at least, for now).

- The key is to keep your links relevant to your users, which will help you to avoid unsubscribes and keep your product at the top of their minds.

- Give it some time and those conversions are bound to start happening sooner or later.

- Who said that email marketing needs to be hard?

CASE STUDY #4
CRAIG MILLER
CHIEF
MARKETING
OFFICER ,
SHOPIFY

"Every Marketer Should Be A Quant"

What once started as a struggling online snowboard store, quickly grew into the most desirable ecommerce platform and has forever changed the ecommerce game. Shopify is now considered the go-to ecommerce solution for small and medium sized businesses, including internationally renowned companies like Tesla and Google. The mission is plain and simple: to make ecommerce easier and more affordable, giving anyone the ability to start their own online store.

What makes Shopify different from other platforms? It is incredibly customizable, offering an extensive array of tools and apps for creating and managing an online store. It also provides unparalleled customer service, granting continuous access to the customer success gurus team 24/7, 365 days a year.

2015 has been a remarkable year for Shopify, boasting one of the best performing technology IPOs and reaching over 200,000 merchant stores with over $1.9 billion worth of orders. Gaining this level of success has been anything but easy and straightforward. In the early years, despite having a good product, growth was slow and Shopify was not on anyone's radar. In 2011, Craig Miller joined Shopify as the Chief Marketing Officer. At the time, Shopify had 15,000 customers, and in his words, "I thought all I needed to do was just take a great product and let people know about it, it would be pretty easy." Finding ways to increase the customer base in a big way became his sole focus.

Craig's first order of business was to rebrand the marketing team by calling it the growth team. The reason behind this was to ensure there was no confusion and that everyone on the team knew exactly what was expected of them - to grow the brand. The team's initial traction goal was to double the userbase from 15,000 merchant stores to 30,000 in one year. Craig's strategy for the team was to focus on weekly improvements, growing the customer base by 2 per cent each week. By focusing on weekly results, the task becomes more manageable and easier to track progress. This strategy was in sharp contrast to the traditional marketing method of putting all your time and effort into only one growth channel and hoping it produces a long term 10 per cent improvement. The traditional approach is not easily repeatable, once it's done, you are back to square one, or attempting to echo the same idea - but everyone knows the sequel is never as good as the original. According to Craig, "it's a lot easier, it's a lot more sustainable to actually just do small incremental improvements each week. And if you can get a good cadence of doing that, building on top of yourself, the compounding effect actually outweighs the big shiny ball."

With a clear strategy in place, focusing on weekly repeatable improvements, Craig and his team set out to double their current customer base.

Run Experiments

You won't know which channels are the best until you start testing them and assess results. For Craig, it was about trying things out, testing as much as possible and learning from them. When they found a channel that worked, they would double down on it and spend a lot more time and effort to optimize it. Early on, Google Adwords was a channel that was very effective. The team started to test which keywords generated more business. At the time, a lot of competing businesses were bidding on the Shopify brand name. To combat this, Craig called up every company he could find and offered them a cease-fire, "you stop bidding on our brand name, and I'll stop bidding on your brand name." With Google Adwords it's important to focus on attribution, being able to determine where the customer came from, and how you can take credit for it. For Craig, this meant focusing their efforts on first-click attribution as opposed to last-click attribution. First-click attribution means, if a user comes to the site through an ad and then comes back organically, the first-click in this case, the ad gets the credit. Using first-click attribution, Craig was able to bid on Shopify but only target people that either don't use them or don't know about them. With the strong results based on first-click traffic, the team began researching into the lifetime value of a customer and acquisition costs, so they could ask for a larger budget. With the larger budget, the team was able to spend more money and get better returns.

Product as Marketing

Your product is your greatest growth hack. This is often overlooked and it certainly was at Shopify. In the early days, there was a belief that the only reason people used competing products was because of their marketing. They had an inferior product but did a better job of attracting customers. According to Craig, "good product is good marketing." The team's early success gave them the freedom to start exploring outside traditional marketing channels. A problem Craig noticed was, "most people have created an artificial invisible line between the product and marketing." People will test ads and tweak the website, but when it comes to the product, they stop experimenting. In his mind, this is a bizarre division of labor. At the time, there was a reluctance to tweak Shopify's product, something that Craig knew had to change in order to grow the business. Craig and his team decided to start changing the on-boarding process through AB testing. Every user was given a number, if the number was even, they would see one screen; if the number was odd, they would see another screen. The team would monitor the data to determine which screen performed better. Another tweak that the growth team made to the product was with the credit card requirement. At the time, Shopify gated the trial of its software by credit card. This requirement was moved to a later step in the process. What the team found was they got a lot more people on-boarded and higher quality leads, people who actually wanted to use the product. At the time, they offered a 30 day trial, however, they dropped it down to 14 days. Most people think this is done to increase the number of users, but it actually had the opposite effect, they slightly decreased. The reason they did a 14 day trial was it gave the team data in two weeks instead of four weeks. They were able to run twice as many tests throughout the year to better determine product performance.

Differentiate yourself from traditional practices

If you continually follow the current marketing trends it can be very difficult to stand out from the crowd. As Craig and his team started exploring other channels, they began to focus on search engine optimization. SEO had become a lightning rod for criticism with many people dismissing it as a viable channel. Rather than follow convention, they took a different approach with SEO. Craig said, "user-generated content is one of the most scalable ways of doing SEO." To leverage user-generated content, a discussion forum was created on Shopify's website. At the time, the common practice was to build your community on Facebook. This made little sense to Craig considering Facebook now owns the communication channel rather than Shopify. With the decision to create their own forum, not only does the company own the content, but Shopify will also rank on search results for those keywords related to its product. This unconventional tactic enabled Shopify to improve their on-page and off site SEO.

Since joining Shopify as the Chief Marketing Officer, Craig and his growth team have managed to double the customer base respectively each year. Craig's continuous commitment to experimenting with channels and product have certainly played a major role in Shopify's success. In Craig's own words, "we're in a fiercely competitive field, so any kind of incremental improvement, be it one or two per cent, if that compounds, that has been huge leverage for us and a huge reason why we are successful."

Craig wants other marketers to take away the following from Shopify's experiences:

Firstly, be weary of traditional marketing practices. "I think there's a lot of conventional wisdom out there, and if you go with conventional wisdom you're going to get average gains." Rather than just follow what others are doing, Craig suggests questioning everything. He routinely questions everything that they do at Shopify. You can't afford to be lazy and simply follow current trends.

Secondly, be willing to fail. Companies talk about being willing to fail, but in reality seldom put this belief into practice with their employees. "At Shopify we had people that within the first week had made major mistakes, and instead of us firing them, those are the people that we congratulated, we praised, we said do more of that." On the flipside, they had people who after a few weeks still had not made any impact, so the discussion became, "maybe this is not the right type of company for you." Instilling a company culture that embraces failure was incredibly important, as Craig highlighted, "make an impact, make a dent in Shopify." When asked how do you give people the freedom to fail Craig said, "I am super transparent. I actually talk a lot about my mistakes and failures."

Finally - test, test, test. This is crucial to growth marketers. Focus on running many experiments. Don't make the common mistake of investing a lot of time and money into a marketing channel that does not produce results. As Craig said, "I think the best way to do things is just run a lot of experiments, do a lot of things...even if a lot of those things fail, you still have a bunch of things that actually do succeed. But when you put all your eggs in one basket, it doesn't work at all." The key as Craig showed, is to get into a cadence of running several tests each week.

33

THE "KEEP THEM SEPARATED" HACK

How to send different traffic sources to different landing pages

THE PHASE:
Launch

DIFFICULTY:
Advanced

WE USE:
Unbounce.com

The Hack: Your landing pages can make or break your marketing campaign. Read that again: MAKE or BREAK. We're talking about any campaign. Whether you're managing AdWords, reaching out to custom audiences on Facebook or remarketing using the Google Display Network. ALL of these promotional methods require well-built landing pages. There's no point in spending money on paid advertising unless your landing page is going to have your back on the conversion front. With AdWords, it's even less optional to have a great landing page as this affects everything: from your cost-per-click to whether your ads will even show in the first place. Paid channels aside, your email campaigns and social promotions also require the services of your high-converting landing page. Once you've acquired the user using any paid or organic channel, activating them comes down to following conversion-centered landing page design best practices. Read below to see how to achieve this.

Now Hack It:

- Have ONE goal for each landing page that you create. Your pages' attention ratio needs to be 1:1, meaning that there shouldn't be more than one link on the page. And that link should be your CTA (call-to-action).

- Your CTA needs to be the starting point for your landing page design and it will change depending on the traffic source of your arriving visitor.

- For each acquisition channel, you need to think how it may affect your landing page:

- Regardless of the channel, Message Match is critical. This refers to how well the call to action messaging matches the content on the landing page

- For Facebook ads, display ads or any other visual ad, you also have to ensure wording of your ad matches the headline and sub-head text on your page design match. This is to do with how well the design of your ad matches the landing page design.

- In addition to considering the acquisition channel, you also need to account for the following:

- While it may seem obvious, the landing page has to display correctly on each device. This is crucial so make sure that your page is either responsive or adaptive. Remember the less they know, the longer the page needs to be!

- The page length will be determined by your visitors' awareness stage.

- Go through Unbounce's 50-point conversion checklist to make you haven't missed anything.

- Also, the aforementioned Unbounce app allows for Dynamic Text Replacement which, together with AdWords' Dynamic Keyword Insertion, lets you change ad and landing page text on the fly to match your user's search query. This feature is truly awesome!

- You are now a growth-hacking landing page expert and with great power comes… The responsibility to activate your users like there ain't no tomorrow!

34

THE PROGRESS HACK

How to create a progress meter to growth hack your customer's attention spans

THE PHASE:
Launch

DIFFICULTY:
Intermediate

WE USE:
Wordpress
plugins

The Hack: Your users are busy. And impatient. And distracted. And have the attention span of a goldfish. Seriously. They're not going to diligently go through each step of your onBOREDing process. They're not... Just get over it. Well, most of them won't but you definitely want them to. Your activation numbers depend on it. So, how do you get your app to hold your users' interest long enough to activate? You have to do something that will keep them glued to the screen, that's how. In short, you need to growth hack your users' attention spans. But it's not as science fiction-like as it sounds. And it definitely doesn't involve brain transplants, lobotomies or strange mechanical contraptions. Just a nice little progress bar for your most crucial activation processes in order to show users where they are in the process (and how little they have to go.)

Now Hack It:

- There are a few names for this: "progress meter," "progress bar," "completeness meter," or our favorite, the "'are we there yet?' indicator". Just kidding, that last one we made up.

- If your front-end website or blog is built on Wordpress then you are in luck. There are many status bar Wordpress plugins you can install

- Outside of Wordpress, you could use jQuery progress meter plugins

- Then again, you can always "roll your own" completeness indicator with the help of a developer.

- Phew! These instructions are now 100% complete.

35

THE 'LET'S MAKE A DEAL' HACK

How to create your own Groupon-like daily deal email to your customers

THE PHASE:
Launch

DIFFICULTY:
Easy

WE USE:
Mailchimp.com
(free to start)

The Hack: Who likes deep discount deals? We do that's who! You don't have to be Groupon (the archbishop of deep discounts) to offer your followers relevant and timely deals. This hack is simple. Search the web for great discount deals that would be relevant to your audience. Put three or four into an email newsletter and voila! Your audience will thank you.

Now Hack It:

- Search Google for daily deals based on the interests of your customers. For example if you sell gardening books, search for gardening deals. You could also setup keyword alerts that'll come straight to your inbox.

- Pick three or four of the daily deals in your niche. Focus on one of the deals with the best product, best reviews and best discount.

- Create a simple and easy newsletter template in MailChimp. Use a template that allows for multiple promotions.

- Populate the newsletters with your deals and send to your newsletter list.

PRO TIP:
You'll want to make sure you're not sending this on a daily basis. While the customers will thank you, they're likely being spammed with multiple emails daily and you don't want your email address or content to be associated with that behavior. If it is, when an important message does go out, it'll be missed.

36

THE RESOURCES PAGE HACK

How to cast a huge content shadow

THE PHASE:
Launch

DIFFICULTY:
Intermediate

WE USE:
UberFlip.com
(starting at
$500/month)

The Hack: There are few buzz words bigger today than "content marketing," but that's because it works. The benefits of content marketing include free inbound traffic, increased SEO presence and becoming an authoritative and trusted source in your industry. Check out our friends at UberFlip – they offer easy to use content hubs that let you content market like the big guys. Easy!

Now Hack It:

- Sign up at for a trial account at UberFlip.com.

- Next you'll want to customize your hub. Create your look and feel by changing colors, logo, header banners etc.

- Start by adding some feeds. You can bring in your Facebook account, Twitter account, blogs, other people's posts and much more.

- Add a small code snippet to your website so UberFlip can add content to it.

- You can pin your most important posts to the top, so that they are always visible and prominent to new visitors.

- Next experiment with adding some lead generation gates. This turns a content tile into a lead generating machine by requiring visitors to fill out a form or providing their email addresses before accessing the content.

PRO TIP:
Set up a feed for your Twitter favorites. Then any time you favorite a tweet, it'll post directly to your hub. Now you can control your web content from your smartphone. Genius right! Now you can work while you're on the go.

37

THE DOLLAR SHAVE HACK

How to hack a subscription e-commerce business

THE PHASE:
Pre Launch

DIFFICULTY:
Intermediate

WE USE:
Cratejoy.com
(Free for 14
days, then $39/
month and 1.25%
+ $0.10 per
transaction)

The Hack: Subscription services are all the rage today, with tons of them popping up to serve the needs of shavers, beer enthusiasts, video game geeks, healthy snack devourers and dog treats for our loyal friends to name a few.

Why are they so hot? For two reasons.

Firstly, companies like Dollar Shave Club have lead the way in showing entrepreneurs how profitable the space can be.

Secondly, recurring revenue rocks. Get one customer instead of six customers for the same price. The larger lifetime value of each customer allows you to spend more on customer acquisition.

Cratejoy is like Shopify, but designed specifically for subscription sales. So the setup is similar, but focused on recurring revenue and recurring promotions.

Now Hack It:

- Set up an account at cratejoy.com.

- Research your niche. You'll want to pick a niche that has lots of customers, monthly search traffic and disposable income. It also needs to make sense as a recurring concept.

- Prepare your product photos and descriptions. These are the key to a beautiful website.

- Select a template. This is the foundation for your web store.

- Add your products and set your delivery schedules. Pay attention to the "cut-off date," the day in which customers switch over to the next month.

- Launch your store and promote it aggressively.

PRO TIP:
Referral programs can be really effective in this space. Try a referral program in which the referrer gets a free month credited for every new customer they bring on!

38

THE E-COMMERCE HACK

How to hack a quick and effective e-commerce store

THE PHASE:
Pre Launch

DIFFICULTY:
Intermediate

WE USE:
Shopify.com (14 days for FREE, $29/month for Basic and $.30 + 2.9% per transaction)

The Hack: Think you've got the next Slap Chop and want to start selling them online? This is the hack for you. When we need a quick and easy e-commerce site, we call on our friends at Shopify to help us get to market quickly. Shopify is the easiest way to quickly and cheaply launch a new e-commerce site. They can handle an onslaught of orders if your product is the next Ab Roller; and if it turns out no one is interested in your gadget, you won't have lost your shirt.

Now Hack It:

- Sign up for free trial at Shopify.com - our favorite e-commerce platform for its ease of use and power.

- Next you'll need to select a template, either free or paid. This is really important because it represents how your site will look when complete. Make sure to select an automatically mobile responsive site, so it looks great on mobile too. This is a non-negotiable in today's market.

- A website is only as good as your content and photos, so pay a lot of attention to your photos, product descriptions, pricing, shipping details. And remember a photo is worth 1000 words so spend a bit of time taking some decent images.

- Begin to build out your template. Start slowly by uploading your products and build out from your product catalog. This will be tricky the first time you attempt it, but will get easier as you get accustomed to the process.

- Set your shipping rates for both domestic and international customers. If you charge sales tax, set the tax rates for each of the regions.

- Once you've tested your store and are happy with it, launch your store and start to promote it. Remember, even though you've spent a ton of time on it, no one knows it exists, so promote aggressively.

PRO TIP:
One of the best features of Shopify is their third party app store. This allows you to quickly and easily add on functionality to your web store. Some of our favorite apps include Chimpified for MailChimp integration, Product Upsell to upsell products at checkout and S Loyalty to create a loyalty program.

39

THE DEMO VIDEO HACK

How to produce a cheap and cheerful product demo video

THE PHASE:
Launch

DIFFICULTY:
Intermediate

WE USE:
QuickTime (free)

The Hack: Video is where it's at in today's marketing environment. Especially if you cater to a younger demographic, many of your visitors would prefer to see your product than read about your product. It's a pretty well-known fact now if you're looking to get noticed on social media, video is the way to do it. Fortunately, producing demo or walkthrough videos has never been easier. In fact, you'll likely already have the software to produce these videos on your laptop (and all this time you didn't even know!).

Now Hack It:

- Almost every PC or Mac has QuickTime on it for watching MP4 and AVI videos. On a Mac it's your default video player in most cases.

- What you didn't know is that it can also produce great quality screen capture videos.

- Start with a script, as it's the most important piece. Figure out what you want to demo and in what order. Write down what you want to highlight. If it helps to draw a storyboard, do that too.

- Launch QuickTime and select new screen recording from the File menu.

- Set the portion of your screen you want to record and click record.

- Walk the customer through the key features of your product or service. Focus on the key features and what sets you apart from your competitors.

- Use your internal microphone to speak directly to the user like you were demoing on the phone. If you don't want to use your own voice, you can get a cheap voice over of your script at voices.com.

- Review your recording and make sure you're happy with it. If you have some basic video skills, you can add some graphics and callouts.

- End the video with a strong call to action.

PRO TIP:
If you want to hack a script, have three or four people in your company record an audio recording of their own walk through. Transcribe all three or four audio recordings and use transcripts to create script. QuickTime has been updated to allow you to record the screen of an iPhone or iPad if you're using a Mac. It's a pretty straightforward process and you'll have the screen of the mobile device up in front of you. Great if your product is an App.

40

THE ANIMATED VIDEO HACK

How to hack an animated explainer video on a budget

THE PHASE:
Pre Launch

DIFFICULTY:
Beginner

WE USE:
Promoshin.com

The Hack: What's a start-up without an animated explainer video? Well it's like a hipster without an instamatic camera! All joking aside, video marketing is extremely popular right now, and customers and investors alike enjoy a quick and effective video to explain your product offering or business model. These videos can get very expensive, especially if you've never produced one before. Have no fear - we're here to save your nerves and your wallet a whole bunch of abuse.

Now Hack It:

- Animated videos can be very complicated projects to manage and can be very expensive.

- Promoshin offers templated videos where you embed your story into a video template. The result is a good looking video that saves you money.

- At Promoshin.com, you'll fill out questionnaire about your business to get their producers started.

- Over the following few weeks, they will send you scripts, concepts, storyboards and samples for your feedback or approval. Feel free to make as many changes as you want until you're satisfied.

- You will also select a voice for the voiceover and background music for the video. You get to select from many different male and female voices.

- When your video is ready it's time to amplify! Promote your video on your homepage, special media, YouTube, Vimeo, Social Media and anywhere else you think your audience will be watching. Even consider putting some promotional budget to amplifying the video on social or YouTube.

PRO TIP:
Spend lots of time and effort on the script, as the key to the video is the script. Keep the video short and sweet, and resist the temptation to try to say everything. The video should leave the viewer feeling like the concept makes sense and with a desire to ask for more.

41

THE HANDWRITTEN HACK

How to send beautiful handwritten notes to your customers

THE PHASE:
Pre Launch

DIFFICULTY:
Easy

WE USE:
HelloBond.com
(about $3/card)

The Hack: It's very common to get start-up advice telling you to do the things that don't scale in the beginning. This makes a lot of sense, because your first 100 or 1000 traction customers are extremely important and extremely challenging to acquire. Once you've got them you don't want to lose or disappoint them. It's a real win when we can apply a personal touch to early adopters AND have a system that scales. Bond will send handwritten notes to your customers, that are created using robots! Welcome to the future, we've been waiting for you.

Now Hack It:

- Are you ready to wow your early adopters? We thought so. Let's go …..

- Head over to bond.co

- Select your stationery style. Pick one of their existing designs or have them make one for you with your logo.

- Select handwriting style and compose your message.

- Upload your contact list and let Bond take care of the rest.

- Their robots will handwrite your notes, in your chosen writing style, and send them off to your customers. They'll never know it wasn't done with your own hand!

PRO TIP:
Take advantage of Bond's API and CRM integrations to automate the sending of customer data from your website to Bond!

42

THE LIVE CHAT HACK

How to offer live chat customer support on your site

THE PHASE:
Launch

DIFFICULTY:
Intermediate

WE USE:
olark.com (free trial, $14/month for one operator) and vmgbpo.com for staffing.

The Hack: We all like the idea of live chat on our websites, as a way to engage with and answer questions from customers, right in the moment. It's a great way to deal with objections fast and even help clear up misunderstandings should you be offering a complicated or detailed service. But tying ourselves to our computer to answer said questions is not an appealing thought. You have two options. Use the page targeting options (offered by the live chat providers) to only offer live chat on key pages and at key times of day. Or outsource the staffing using this hack.

Now Hack It:

- Sign Sign-up for free trial of olark.

- Create a detailed FAQ with up to 40 key customer service questions.

- Engage VMG on their basic $250/month 24/7 staffing package.

- You'll get a non-dedicated agent manning your live chat 24 hours a day.

- They'll use your FAQs to provide information and links to customers, based on their chat query

PRO TIP:
Use the chat reports to search for new FAQs and refine existing FAQs that aren't being proven effective. Also, if you're not ready for VMG then do it yourself. The feedback you'll receive will help you create a better customer experience and will set you up to provide better answers when you're ready to move to a service like VMG. Also remember that #42 is the answer to the ultimate question of life, the universe and everything.

43

THE ANALYTICS 101 HACK

How to use Quill Engage to get your feet wet in analytics

THE PHASE:
Launch

DIFFICULTY:
Beginner

WE USE:
QuillEngage.com
(FREE)

The Hack: To some degree, the success of your marketing depends on your ability to interpret your analytics data to make good decisions. But learning analytics is hard and takes time. You can dip your toe in the analytics pool and get hit by a fire hose! Don't fret, as you start diving into analytics, you'll get better quickly. In the meantime, you can use a great tool called Quill Engage to get a simple snapshot of your analytics, with simple tips on how to improve.

Now Hack It:

- Sign up for free account with Quill Engage.

- Follow the instructions to authorize your Google Analytics account.

- Every month you'll receive simple, visual reports illustrating changes in your analytics and tips to improve.

PRO TIP:
At some point you'll want to improve your analytics game and grow out of Quill. Looking for the quickest way? Get analytics certified for free with Google's training program found at http://www.google.com/analytics/learn/index.html

44

THE CONTENT FACTORY HACK

How to use Text Broker to turbocharge your content production

THE PHASE:
Launch

DIFFICULTY:
Intermediate

WE USE:
Textbroker.com
(from 1.3 to 7.2
cents per word.
We use the 4
star 2.4 cents/
word option)

The Hack: This is one of Jeff's favorite hacks at Borrowell and he uses it to create a content production engine that blasts their content game into the stratosphere. Most of the time, it's best to focus on high quality, consumer-centric, evergreen style content, because the 80/20 rule suggests that 20% of your content will drive 80% of your content traffic. But there's something to be said for good, old-fashioned content velocity, blogs on blogs, dripping with keywords and links. We don't always have the time or resources to spend on each and every blog post, and that's where Textbroker comes in. Harness the power of their crowd and post writing gigs to their marketplace. You'll have good, fast and cheap blog posts returned to you in hours or days, for only pennies per word. Just promise us you won't tell anyone about this great hack…

Now Hack It:

- Register for an account at textbroker.com – make sure you select a "client" account and not an "author" account.

- You need to deposit funds into your account before you place your first order. You can deposit with PayPal, and $25 should get you started.

- Select an "open order" and fill out the form to request your content. You can select the quality level you need, the turnaround time and brief the author.

- Authors will request the gig and you can select who you want to write for you. Once it's complete, you'll be notified and can review the post, approve or suggest changes. Once you complete a few orders, you can request specific authors who you've worked with in the past.

PRO TIP:
Rumor has it that Google doesn't like duplicate content, so we think twice before using the same blog post in multiple locations, lest we get penalized by the Google bots. Use Textbroker to re-write your posts and fear duplicate content no more. Look at you go, you growth hacker!

CASE STUDY #5 ANUM HUSSAIN SENIOR GROWTH MARKETER, HUBSPOT AND SIDEKICK

B2C2B

Deep in the heart of Hubspot lies a covert group of marketing and product SEALS who loosely call themselves Hubspot Labs – a group that CTO Dharmesh Shah calls a "super-secret R&D group." Hubspot Labs' projects get seed funding and support from Hubspot, but treats its projects like start-ups and expects them to develop and commercialize on their own two feet.

Hubspot Labs' greatest hit to date has been Sidekick, a nifty email tracking tool that lets you track the flight of your sales email and delivers CRM type intelligence right into your email client. For example, a Gmail user on Google Chrome can install the Sidekick chrome extension and get this tracking and CRM built right into Gmail. Sidekick prices itself as a freemium product, meaning you get it free for 200 tracks a month, and then it shuts off, or you ante up $10/month for unlimited use. Most salespeople who value real time data are sold, and consider the paid account a good investment.

According to Sidekick Senior Growth Marketer Anum Hussain, "Sidekick's first traction goal was 100,000 users." A team of ten, featuring three growth marketers and seven product developers, Anum set out to understand the buying pattern of the customers, test sales channels to limit wasted time and resources, and use data science to determine the best course of action for their acquisition challenges.

Anum's "a-ha moment" came when she tried to figure out why her early acquisition activities weren't leading to conversions. "That was when our eyes opened to the problem: Sidekick isn't a B2B product. It's not a B2C product either. It's instead a part of what the industry is calling the 'consumerization of IT'. It's B2C2B."

We all know about B2C and B2B but what the heck is B2C2B? Anum best describes B2C2B with a quote from venture capitalist Tomasz Tunguz that B2C2B is about "winning the hearts and minds of the intermediate consumer, the employees of a customer". The way this works is fascinating: during user acquisition, customer adopts the product for free and begins using. As she experiences success with it, her colleagues catch on and sign-up for free accounts themselves. Once the team starts benefiting from it, they're no longer satisfied with the free version, and lobby for their manager to purchase premium version for the team. A B2B sale is made as a result of a B2C trial.

So using this strategy of freemium pricing and a B2C2B mindset, Sidekick set out to acquire their first 100,000 users, and here's how they did it:

Commit to Experimentation

Companies never know where their best users are going to come from, and the ones that do are often wrong and waste a lot of time and resources. Anum committed her team to focus on experimentation and began with a list of five channels they thought could work. "While best practices can inspire us," explained Anum, "every decision we make should stem from an experiment. "For example, the Sidekick team hypothesized that they could get conversions from LinkedIn. They ran a small LinkedIn Pulse test, estimating that they could acquire 200 users for the small investment. This result would give credibility to the channel and suggest that further testing and optimizing were necessary. However, the test only led to 21 signups. "Once we have that data, we simply rinse and repeat for every channel."

Use Data to Drive Decisions

This may be a common theme already, but Anum's take on the practice proved very interesting. Inspired by the massive resource guides produced by HelpScout (and wooed by their insane SEO performance, ranking above Wikipedia!)she decided to create their own content heavy, SEO focused resource pages they called Site Pages. The result is that the six site pages they created caused their organic traffic to increase 10% week over week, effectively doubling their organic traffic every six weeks! Anum doubled down on this success by adding top performing and topical blog posts to the site pages, and creating landing pages on steroids that created leverage by providing free traffic into the future.

Use Technology to Transition from Experimentation to Scale

As Anum began to uncover channels that showed signs of promise, her new challenge shifted to scaling the success and proving that it could be a predictable, repeatable channel. She explained "Experiments got us to the right channels. Authentic measurement helps us monitor success. And digging into the data helps us move in faster, more impactful ways. That leaves scalability". Using the example of customer onboarding, Anum explained how they conducted over 60 experiments to determine which onboarding process lead to the highest retention.

When you sign-up to a blog subscription, you typically leave your email address, confirm your email address and then begin receiving the next blog post in sequence. While commonplace, this onboarding process is impersonal and a waste of a valuable touch point. "With that question in mind, I began running our own content onboarding experiments to better understand how we can give our readers immense value upon sign-up to retain them as monthly active subscribers for an extended period of time. "Instead of sending the next sequence blog post, Anum put subscribers on a drip campaign, sending them their best performing content over the course of the four weeks. This resulted in click through rates that were 2x bigger than the regular email sequence. Plus, it could all be automated using email marketing automation, so it scaled efficiently.

So what would Anum like marketers to learn from Sidekick's experiences?

Firstly, do the work. "You need to do the grunt work. When you're experimenting, you need to do the tedious work that needs to be done. Resources will come when the results come. Every single week we were expected to present the results from the experiments. If you didn't, it suggested that you weren't doing the grunt work."

Secondly, she provides amazing insight into the difficult task of determining when and where to apply best practices versus charting your own course. "Avoid blindly following best practices and focus instead on uncovering what works best for your own audience."

Finally, and of crucial importance to growth marketers is chasing what she calls "authentic growth," which is done by ensuring that you're measuring and optimizing for the right key performance metric. Sidekick tracked the number of Weekly Active Users as a proxy for their users getting value from the product every week. "It's far too easy to get caught up in vanity metrics – push you or your team to pursue meaningful metrics for authentic growth."

45

THE DEJA VU HACK

How to use retargeting to stay in front of your customers

THE PHASE:
Launch

DIFFICULTY:
Advanced

WE USE:
AdWords.com (retarget on websites) or AdRoll.com (retarget websites and Facebook)

The Hack: Just because a web visitor isn't ready to purchase TODAY doesn't mean they won't be ready to purchase down the road. The problem is, how do you stay top of mind for them after they leave your site? The simplest way is through retargeting advertising. Ever wonder why you visited a site one day and then saw their banner ad the next? This isn't a coincidence, these very rarely happen in the modern world. Ever wonder how the local start-up can afford to advertise on the Wall Street Journal site? It's actually easier than you might think. The answer – retargeting ads.

Now Hack It:

- You'll need to be driving traffic to your site already. Without a decent amount of traffic, you can't effectively retarget.

- If you're advertising exclusively on AdWords, use them for retargeting. If you're also spending money on Facebook, consider AdRoll for their ability to jump the fence between websites and Facebook.

- Add a retargeting campaign to your AdWords program (display network only).

- To set up your campaign, they will ask you to install a retargeting pixel to your website. Don't worry, this is actually a pretty easy task to get sorted.

- You will be sent a small amount of code to install on your website, as well as instructions on how to do it. You've got a couple of choices here, namely DIY or PSE. Either send to your webmaster, or follow the instructions on how to install yourself. If your site is hosted on any of the major platforms, installing code is pretty easy.

- Now customers that visit your site will get a "cookie" that follows them around the web, and shows them your ad on participating sites (80%+ of all websites).

PRO TIP:
AdRoll is great because they'll retarget to websites AND Facebook, so you can serve ads to past visitors on their Facebook feed. Spend $100/week and they'll even design your ads for you! You can also upload a list of email addresses and target them specifically on websites!

46

THE QUALITY SCORE HACK

How to lower your cost per click by hacking Google's quality score

THE PHASE:
Launch

DIFFICULTY:
Intermediate

WE USE:
AdWords.com

The Hack: When it comes to Google advertising, quality score is everything. It determines where your ad appears and how much you'll pay for it, among other things. Improving quality score can reduce your per click costs by up to 50%, translating into an 80% reduction in cost per acquisition (otherwise known as Marketing Nirvana). An average quality score is 5, and let's face it, no one wants to be average. Shoot for an 8 or 9.It's the difference between rolling a boulder uphill versus downhill. Get your hack on and aim for Nirvana!

Now Hack It:

- Many different things can impact your quality score, both in-ad and on-page.

- There are tactics that can be used to increase your quality score inside the AdWords dashboard.

- Ad extensions are a free and an easy way to put your ads on steroids.

- Add site links. Site links can be added for free and they increase the physical presence of your Google ad, by giving searchers more detailed links to navigate directly to.

- Add review extensions if you have received positive news pieces. You can quote or paraphrase a favorable line from the article, then link your listing with an extra line from the review. If your review quote is clicked, it takes the searcher to the review, at no cost to you. It also increases credibility of the ad.

- Create an ad group called "branded keywords" and add all the keywords associated with your brand name, website name, and variations and misspellings. It's counterintuitive to want searchers to click on your paid link versus your organic link. But these ads get click through rates of 50%+, which will increase your overall account CTR (a major contributor to Quality Score).

PRO TIP:
Don't add too many extensions or extensions that aren't appropriate (i.e. – a phone number extension if you don't want phone calls).Google decides which extensions to serve, so we don't want to give them too many choices.

47

THE GMAIL HACK

How to use Gmail Sponsored Promotions to infiltrate your customers inbox

THE PHASE:
Launch

DIFFICULTY:
Advanced

WE USE:
AdWords.com

The Hack: Ever logged into your Gmail account, clicked on the "promotions" tab and seen those little ads at the top of your inbox? If not, give it a go! You'll be amazed. Guess what my friend, those ads are served based on the content of your email! I know, right? When a user clicks the ad, it expands to a big 650x650 graphic of your design. Let's use this to our advantage.

Now Hack It:

- GSP is currently in beta, so you must request access. If you really want to launch these, and can't get access, try using a Google Preferred agency, who might be able to help

- The ad type you're looking for is called "Display Network Only – All Features"

- Under ad targeting options, select "use different targeting method," select "placements" and add "mail.google.com" to the placements.

- Create your ads under the "ads" tab. You'll need a good looking 650 x 650 pixel graphic for this ad type. If you don't have the resources to produce this, try Fiverr or 99designs (see our hacks on these options).

- Now you can add the keywords you want to target then launch and test your new ads.

PRO TIP:
You can add specific domain names as keywords (hello competitors!).

48

THE TV COMMERCIAL HACK

How to use YouTube video ads when you can't afford TV ads

THE PHASE:
Launch

DIFFICULTY:
Intermediate

WE USE:
YouTube.com/yt/
advertising

The Hack: Can't afford TV ads? (Do people still watch those?) Try YouTube ads. They're actually better! They're cheaper, you can target your audience better, you only pay if a viewer interacts and you can change them out daily - try doing that with traditional TV advertising. If you have a compelling video, consider turning it into a catchy ad.

Now Hack It:

- •Start by creating a great thirty second video. Make sure it meets YouTube's specifications, you don't want your hard work to go to waste.

- Four types of ads:

  - In-Stream (before a video, skip-able after five seconds, pay if they watch thirty seconds)

  - In-Slate (shown beginning of long videos, only pay when ad is watched)

  - In-Search (shown next to search results)

  - In-Display (shown on websites that embed YouTube video ads)

- Upload a video. Pay special attention to title, keywords and descriptions.

- Target your audience based on many attributes including demographics, keywords and interests.

- Set your budget and launch your ad. Test multiple calls to action, titles, etc. to optimize over time

PRO TIP:
YouTube Video Promotion option lets you pay to promote your video in search results. Not nearly as competitive as Google search.

49

THE DAY-PART
HACK

How to use AdWords' bid multipliers
to get better traffic quality

THE PHASE:
Launch

DIFFICULTY:
Advanced

WE USE:
Adwords.com

The Hack: You've been a good marketer, and you've been on top of your data, diligently searching for trends in the data that can lead to optimizations. If you're lucky, you'll have found some trends worth testing, but what exactly do you do with this knowledge? Well you'll want to start using bid multipliers in AdWords to quickly test trends in the data, leading to more profitable clicks. After all, the more profitable the click the better it is for everyone!

Now Hack It:

- Measure which of these attributes have an effect on your cost per acquisition:

  - Day of week

  - Time of day

  - Geographic location

  - Device type (desktop, mobile, tablet)

- See any trends? Good. Let's exploit them.

- Use AdWords bid multipliers to bid more for attributes that lead to lower CPAs and less on attributes that don't.

- Multipliers work on a plus or minus percentage, so if you want to increase bids by 25% for Mondays, multiply Monday by +25%.If you want to decrease mobile traffic by 50%, multiply mobile by -50% (the only current way to completely remove mobile is by multiplying mobile by -100%)

- In the example above, AdWords will bid more for profitable days and less for unprofitable devices.

PRO TIP:
If you have a physical location, use bid multipliers to bid much more for searchers closer to your location. 66% of searchers will visit a business after a local search.

50

THE 'HAVE YOUR PEOPLE CALL MY PEOPLE' HACK

How to use Google's mobile Adwords call button to drive lead volume

THE PHASE:
Launch

DIFFICULTY:
Intermediate

WE USE:
Adwords.com

The Hack: When Google released their mobile ad call button, they stated in a press release that 70% of mobile searches terminate with a phone call. So basically, with all this innovation, searchers are using their phones and the internet as replacements for the more traditional Yellow Pages or Directory Assistance. This is great news if you're a business looking for phone leads. The call to action in the ad is a button that initiates a phone call, and you pay for the call, not the click.

Now Hack It:

- Select the appropriate ad group in AdWords.

- Select "call only" ads.

- Create your call only ad like you would any other AdWords ad.

- Ensure that the call phone number is listed somewhere on your website, as Google will not approve the ad otherwise.

- When the searcher clicks the button, the advertiser is charged and the call is placed (regardless if the call is completed).

PRO TIP:
If you use the Google forwarding phone number, powered by Google Voice, you can set up conversion tracking for phone calls of a certain duration.

51

THE 'INTRO TO REDDIT' HACK

How to acquire customers on HackerNews and Reddit

THE PHASE:
Launch

DIFFICULTY:
Intermediate

WE USE:
Reddit

The Hack: You may be an avid reader of Reddit or Hacker News (HN) but do you actively use these sites to promote your app? Most likely the answer is a big fat "NO." Don't worry, you're not the only one guilty of this growth hacking blasphemy. After all, it's not that different to getting sick of drinking your own coffee as a barista. Or something like that…But the good news is that it's not too late to make a course correction and tap into these awesome communities to acquire early adopters. This will particularly pay large dividends if your product's user base overlaps with the psycho-demographics of these sites' audiences. Also, remember that tech journalists and other tech glitterati frequent both of these often. As a result, if you get it right, you could strike publicity gold. Read on to learn how to effectively pimp your wares on these niche sites.

Now Hack It:

- For both sites, the key is to tailor your content:

- If you're posting to Reddit, then add something along the lines of "Dear Redditors"

- HN readers aren't as love with themselves (sorry, Redditors) so the ego-stroking to the title (feel free to get creative)may not have to be as strong here. But as always, a bit of "caring before sharing" goes a long way.

- For HN, turn your post title into a clickable link to your website, which will help with driving traffic to your site and can help you to get on the front page

- For Reddit, it also pays to address the sub-Reddit specifically and somehow reference something relevant to the group

- In the title, ask people to "Upvote" your post

- In the post itself, add a picture in your post. The goofier the better.

- Next, write a catchy headline and then get "spamming" by asking everyone you know to Upvote it

- Respond to all of the comments (even from the haters as Reddit has plenty of those) and watch your street cred grow.

- But it's not all about HN and Reddit. Depending on your app, there are numerous other communities online that could be perfect for promoting your app: Inbound.org, GrowthHackers.com, etc.

- The moral of the story is to search for online communities that are relevant to your product and then engaging with them in a genuine way.

52

THE CREEPY LINKEDIN HACK

How to use LinkedIn's creepy visitor tracking code to acquire customers

THE PHASE:
Launch

DIFFICULTY:
Intermediate

WE USE:
LinkedIn Premium

The Hack: LinkedIn is a powerful social network that is often underutilized in growth hacking circles and is often ignored by SaaS start-ups in favor of other networks. However, LinkedIn provides a lot of interesting options for acquiring customers. With a user base of 330+ million professionals, you would be foolish to ignore this as a growth hacker. One unique feature of this network is the ability to track other LinkedIn users who view your profile. This is something that neither Facebook nor Twitter provide. As a growth hacker, you definitely want to make use of this. One way of "hacking" this feature is by implementing a bit of code on your website that allows you to see which LinkedIn users visited. For this to work, the user has to be logged into their account and you need to have a paid LinkedIn Premium account. With these two conditions met, you could have a very powerful tool in your marketing arsenal.

Now Hack It:

- Register for a LinkedIn Premium account. The cheapest option is the "Job Seeker" account, which still lets you see who's viewed your profile

- Add the following HTML code somewhere into the <body> tag of your page: "<img src="https://www.linkedin.com/profile/view?authToken=XXauthType=name&id=XX" />a. Here, XX represents your LinkedIn ID page

- Now logged-in LinkedIn users who visit your website will show up in your profile on the "Who's Viewed Your Profile" page. Magic!

53

THE ZUCKERBERG HACK

How to use Spot.im to start your own social network

THE PHASE:
Launch

DIFFICULTY:
Advanced

WE USE:
Spot.im

The Hack: Facebook-schmacebook. When was the last time it did anything for your start-up? Sure, the uber-network helps you to talk to users directly and acquire new customers using its marketing tools. But it always costs you a pretty penny, doesn't it? Ultimately, it is not a channel that you own and everything that you do on the network helps to grow Facebook and Facebook alone. It is rented space. And the rent will keep going up as long as "supply and demand" swings in a network's favor. The same goes for Twitter, LinkedIn, G+ and any other proprietary platform where your audiences live. "But that is the nature of social media," you argue. It's not like you can go and build your own network from scratch. Well, do we have an early Christmas present for you! There IS now a way to create your own social network - read on to find out how.

Now Hack It:

- Creating your own social network - now THAT is one Mega Hack. I mean, we all know how much time and effort the titans of social media have invested into their own networks - *cough* BILLIONS *choke* of dollars *cough*, and just as many lines of code.

- So, creating your own social network seems almost too utopian to be true, right?

- Wrong! All thanks to a visionary start-up, Spot.IM, having an owned media channel that is also your very own social network is within the reach of your eager little hands.

- To make it even more exciting, instead of having to write millions of lines of code, you have to write none. Copy. Paste. Done.

- Ta-da! You now have your own social network. Not as cool as owning your own private tropical island but, hopefully, you'll now have more people to talk to.

- Growth hacking can be a lonely place...

- Alrighty, Facebook, justice has now been served. Now smile because your user retention rates have just skyrocketed!

- (But don't go deleting your Facebook Page just yet).

54

THE LOOKALIKE HACK

How to create lookalike audiences on Facebook to attract the right visitors

THE PHASE:
Launch

DIFFICULTY:
Advanced

WE USE:
Facebook.com or
AdEspresso.com
(see Ad Espresso
hack)

The Hack: One of the most powerful advertising tools in all the land is Facebook lookalike audiences. Facebook allows advertisers to "tell" them what their perfect customers looks like, and then produces a massive lookalike audience based on the user behavior of the ideal customers. Strangely invasive? Yes. Hugely effective? You better believe it.

Now Hack It:

- In Facebook ad manager or in Ad Espresso, select "create audience" and then select "create lookalike audience."
- You have three choices on how to define your ideal customer:
- Create a lookalike audience based on your Facebook page fans.
- Create a lookalike audience based on an uploaded email list of all your best customers.
- Create a lookalike audience based on a conversion pixel that you put on your site. (This is awesome because your custom audience will expand in real-time as visitors hit your pixel).
- For any source, the more sample data you have, the better the lookalike list will be.
- It can take up to 24 hours to create your audience. Once it's created you can set campaigns to target that look alike list.

PRO TIP:
You can do the same process to create a negative lookalike list, based on examples of your worst customers. Then you can target your positive lookalike audience and exclude your negative lookalike audience at the same time! Multitask like a demon.

55

THE TWITTER CARD HACK

How to increase leads, subscribers, and sales directly through Twitter cards.

THE PHASE:
Launch

DIFFICULTY:
Intermediate

WE USE:
Twitter.com (free
to offer to your
own followers, or
you can pay
to promote)

The Hack: We LOVE Twitter lead cards. And our love for them is for a number of reasons. But the biggest reason we love them is because they make it really easy for a lead to engage with you, with no need for friction-y conversions or clicks. These cards are graphical Twitter ad units in which the call to action is to submit your email address in exchange for the content offered. By clicking one button, the lead submits their email address to you.

Now Hack It:

- Create an advertising account with Twitter at ads.twitter.com.

- In "card manager" create a new lead generation card.

- Create an 800 x 200 pixel ad graphic for your card.

- Follow the prompts to create your ad and save your card.

- Now go into the dashboard and create a new campaign, setting the targeting you like. Sometimes it's effective to promote the card to a number of your competitor's followers.

- Select the card you created and launch it.

- Every time someone clicks the button, you will receive their email address. You can export the email list from the ad dashboard.

PRO TIP:
You can automate the Twitter card leads to flow into Drip or MailChimp so you don't have to export them manually. Once in Drip, you can set up a drip campaign for this list and start marketing to them immediately on a set schedule.

56

THE 'SHARING IS CARING' HACK

How to use AddThis to customize share buttons and encourage sharing

THE PHASE:
Launch and
Optimize

DIFFICULTY:
Intermediate

WE USE:
AddThis

The Hack: When was the last time that you ended up on a blog that had a number of social sharing options…Except the one that you prefer? This is one of those few times that you actually decided to share something straight from someone's blog with no way of doing so. Talk about a loss for the author! Or the blog had a million-and-one sharing buttons… All with zero shares next to them. Which straight away takes away from the credibility of the article and makes most users much less likely to share it. Social proof, or the lack of it, tends to have a powerful effect on our choices in life. Even if they're as small as sharing an article online.

When it comes to social sharing buttons, neither too many nor too few is a good look. But with users' social network preferences being so diverse, how do you strike a middle ground? How do you help visitors shout about your blog from their figurative rooftops? Here's a way to hack this.

Now Hack It:

- To sweeten the deal even further, this hack involves a ready-made solution.

- All you have to do is grab the AddThis plugin, install the JavaScript code on your website and away you go.

- To make things even better-er, AddThis will now look at the other cookies on a website and then display the visitor's preferred social sharing buttons.

- We know! How cool is that? And it involves very little effort on your part.

- Now that's what we call growth hacking!

CASE STUDY #6
MARIE NICOLA
BLOGGER, NAT
AND MARIE

GOING VIRAL "Let's see what happens if we..."

In the classic political satire 'Wag the Dog', the following exchange of dialogue between Conrad Brean (played by the indomitable Robert De Niro) and a US presidential aide, John Levy brilliantly sums up what it means to think and act viral –

Conrad Brean: Why is the President in China?

John Levy: Trade Relations

Conrad Brean: You're goddamn right, and it has nothing to do with the B-3 Bomber!

John Levy: There is no B-3 bomber.

Conrad Brean: I just said that! There is no B-3 bomber, and I don't know why these rumors get started!

Now, while Marie 'Karmacake' Nicola of Karmacake.com & SweetGif.com isn't out saving POTUS (just yet), she does know to save a good idea from being lost in the noise and make it go viral in a hurry. Her blog on Karmacake.com is an eclectic commentary spanning various facets of Internet subcultures. Sweetgif is an event based digital photo booth that creates animated gifs instead of traditional paper images which can be uploaded to the Internet for people to view, comment and share them on virtually any social media site, seconds after the image is taken.

Marie is also the host of 'Nat & Marie', Canada's (arguably the Internet's) first weekly live streaming talk show about Internet culture, news and trends. At the time, they were considered authorities in trending online content and had a solid theory about what the 'magic mix' was when it came to viral content.

When the video project came to Marie (a freelance digital strategist at the time) from a mutual friend and The Stellas (Lennon and Maisy's parents), the goal was to see if she could use the resources of Nat and Marie to make the video go viral. According to Marie, "Our goal (for viral success) was defined as a video with over 1 million views associated with it".

Keeping content alive is your first priority

There's a reason we use the adjective 'organic' when dealing with certain kinds of content. It's because, just like anything organic, if unattended for too long, it will die. As Marie puts it, "The half-life of a tweet is 20 minutes while the half-life of a Facebook post is just 90 minutes."

Plus, if this was to be a successful social experiment, there absolutely couldn't be any paid media behind it. Marie knew that once the video was posted, they had a very short window of time to get views and essentially keep the video alive.

With all this in mind, Marie began by posting on all the usual channels with a focus on driving views back to the YouTube video. But the linchpin in this process turned out to be Reddit. Getting to the front page would definitely take more than one post. So, Marie experimented with a couple of different posts to see which one would gain the required traction and do it fast.

"Yes, you do need good content but no one will see that content if you don't get them to click in to the post in the first place" she clearly states.

Aim to build street cred

The Internet may have connected us in multiple ways and brought the global community closer than ever before. But that doesn't mean we're all friends. New content still has to go out on the playground and try to be noticed. And this means saying the right things, being seen by the right people and being in the right places.

On the Internet, the holy grail of being noticed is Reddit's front page. But they couldn't just rock up and ask to be featured. You had to earn your spot. This meant taking a long, hard look at the language being used. Was it compelling enough to pique interest? Was it quirky enough to be noticed?

As Marie explains, "…at the time, the mean age of a Redditor was 16. The importance of the copy in the link was (and still is) critical to the overall success of making it to the (Reddit's) front page."

So how did Marie ensure the copy was going to do the trick? By trolling Redditors a little, with a post that read "Maybe the next generation actually does have some talent. Reddit, I present to you, Lennon & Maisy"

In this case, 'Next Generation' could've been a 16 year old talking about a hilarious baby or someone older failing at being relevant. The ambiguity of the phrase led to many interesting reactions and eventually did the job of getting the video noticed.

As Marie now remembers, "…they hated me, kind of liked the video, got it to the front page and gave me the fodder I needed to spread it across the web." This is the type of street cred you can't buy; you just have to earn it.

Know where journalists shop for stories

Just like the rules of street cred have remained largely unchallenged, the work patterns of journalists have remained consistent too. Merely shifting the process to the Internet, journalists still maintain a beat for information. For the success of our video, (and any organic content) it was important to know wherethey were going. Once we had the hot spots mapped out, our job was to get the video up on those sites and get the story covered. "Reddit was just the first step for us. Once we got there, we quickly moved to all those 'feeder sites' to get the next tier of coverage" Marie explains.

If it has to go viral, it has to travel fast

The importance of this cannot be overstated. If you want to go viral, you have to do it fast because the window is very short. Marie had a team of 4-5 people help her for about 12 hours until the episode of Nat & Marie went to air at 9pm. Their sole focus was literally to get the content to go viral, which was clearly no easy task. "We had to analyze the video, determine the best course of action and execute within the first 2 hours of me being asked to help market the video. It was insane, but it was a day I won't forget!" Marie recalls.

The results spoke loud and clear

The success of the campaign rested not only on the quality of the content in the video but understanding the potential within that video to reach the right target. And Marie claims this is not always a guaranteed thing - "I've seen videos take years before they get discovered and hit and we didn't have years."

In fact, success didn't just come in under a year; it came in just under 48 hours! With over a million views in two days the girls were quick to be interviewed first by Newsweek then spreading to Good Morning America, Ellen and it just kept snowballing from there.

So, what lessons does Marie have for marketers from this successful example?

Firstly, "don't be afraid to talk about compensation. Tomorrow isn't guaranteed and neither is your compensation. Don't assume anything - people who want you to be happy won't ever have a problem with that. Compensation could be money, a trade of services, etc. It's a little slice of something that they have that you would like - high fives also work. We all want gratitude this is just you voicing to your client/friend/friend-of-a-friend what that looks like to you."

Secondly, one needs to be aware of what not achieving goals would look like. This takes courage and determination. "Stand on that precipice and look down - do you want to fall? If not, what do you do to avoid that? Once you have that strategy, then JUMP!" Marie personally loves putting marketing and business plans because she is well aware that without them, it's easy to fall off the edge. And once you do, trying to climb back up to ledge of success is nearly impossible.

Finally, Marie has some strong words for young marketers, "You're only as good as your last success. So as soon as one is done, you're working on the next." She believes in knowing where she wants to go and mapping how each success will contribute to her goal.

"When you break that chain you could be starting from square one again, this makes success so hard to sustain! If that does happen, don't get discouraged just keep on going!" Great advice Marie! Maybe we need to pin that up on desks to remind us.

57

THE NAKED HACK

How to increase early engagement by making your financials transparent

THE PHASE:
Launch

DIFFICULTY:
Intermediate

WE USE:
Our courage

The Hack: "OMG – You're totally naked! I mean, your start-up is totally naked!"

"Dude! We can TOTALLY see all your financial bits."

"Your MRR looks pretty gross by the way. And you seem to have accumulated some fat around your COCA. Go join a growth hacking gym or something!"

"Hey, is that a gray hair on your cLTV?"

"No, you really need to join a growth hacking gym… Actually, with such high churn rate levels, you'll probably end up in a start-up accelerator sooner rather than later."

"It was pretty brave of you to let it all hang out like that, by the way. We'll give you that! Kudos, man!"

"Thanks for the support… Douchebags! Hopefully the shareholders and investors won't take this the wrong way. I mean, we're definitely not a bunch of flashers here or anything. Just a bunch of guys who believe in transparency."

WHAT. Was. That. All. About? Read below to find out how you can hack your financial reporting

Now Hack It:

- This hack calls for a disclosure: it may not grow your revenue straight away. Or, potentially, ever.

- However, it's not out of the question that it may contribute to revenue growth in some indirect way in the future.

- It could even substantially do so depending on the start-up that you have.

- So, what's all this commotion about then? Well, publicly exposing your financial metrics to the world is the new hip thing in Silicon Valley.

- Now the real question is, are you brave enough to do the same?

- It does take some cojones to show your financials for all of the world to see. But then again, sharing is caring.

- And what have you really got to lose? Unless, of course, you're a growing start-up and the whole "size matters" thing bothers you.

- However, it's a good way to act as if you've already hit the big time.

- Think of it as a role-play for your eventual Unicorn club membership.

- Now, if you could just get to $5k MRR before the seed money runs out then you'll be well on your way!

58

THE MAGIC
CLICK HACK

How to use 'click to Tweet' style links
to encourage and incentivize sharing

THE PHASE:
Anytime

DIFFICULTY:
Beginner

WE USE:
ShareLinkGenera-
tor.com

The Hack: We recently discovered a simple and free website that
allows us to create links that automatically populate social media
shares or referral emails. Using these links, we can make it really
easy for customers to share our message with our own crafted
content. Very easy to execute so test it now and test it often.

Now Hack It:

- Visit sharelinkgenerator.com.

- Select the type of link you'd like to create. You can choose from things like Facebook, Twitter, Google +, LinkedIn, Pinterest and Email.

- Use the simple forms to populate the content of your share links.

- Click "create the link" - this will provide you with your customized share link. Anyone who clicks this link will be prompted to auto-share your message.

PRO TIP:
Use the "bcc" functionality on the email share generator links to create referral programs that BCC you. You can reply to the BCC with exclusive content and can track who's sharing and how much. There is a hack a little further in that takes this service to the next level.

59

THE MAKING-FACEBOOK-ADS-EASY HACK

How to use AdEspresso to easily create, launch and test Facebook ads

THE PHASE:
Anytime

DIFFICULTY:
Intermediate

WE USE:
AdEspresso.com (14 days free. The $49/month for up to $3000 monthly spend, $149/month up to $10,000 monthly spend and $299/month up to $25,000 monthly spend).

The Hack: One of our all-time favorite tools is called Ad Espresso. It is a Facebook ad platform that makes it easy to buy Facebook advertising and optimize them into profitable ads. By performing dozens of micro-optimizations in the background, you can focus on the big picture experimentation and let Ad Espresso optimize for creative and copy. Extremely effective, don't tell your friends! We'll keep this a secret between just us.

Now Hack It:

- Sign up for a trial account with Ad Espresso.

- Connect your Facebook account.

- Place ads, set your targeting, set your budget and create your ads, just like you'd do on Facebook's native ad platform.

- Ad Espresso will run tons of small experiments in the background and provide you with actionable optimization advice. If you accept their advice, it's one click to change all affected ads and re-allocate budget to the best performing ads.

PRO TIP:
As you learned in our case study, Ad Espresso has gotten huge through content marketing. Take advantage of their high quality Facebook advertising content. It is some of the best and most actionable Facebook advertising advice on the net.

60

THE SOCIAL MEDIA PLAN HACK

How to hack a social media marketing plan

THE PHASE:
Anytime

DIFFICULTY:
Intermediate

WE USE:
Apps like Buffer and HootSuite will automate the posting, but don't let the automation slow down your plan, as it's the plan that's the most important.

The Hack: You KNOW you need to be active on social media, but you have NO idea how, when or what. Don't worry, you're not alone on that boat, in fact you're onboard a pretty big cruise ship! Most social media marketers will admit to operating on an ad hoc basis, updating profiles when the time permits, and sharing content without a strategy or specific theme. The better approach is to plan out your social media, one month at a time. Here's how we'd recommend getting started.

Now Hack It:

- Create social media calendars one month in advance as a minimum, but don't work too far in advance either, you never know what's around the corner and you don't want to be posting inappropriate content, and you'll always have 30 days of content on hand.

- In the beginning, you can use an Excel spreadsheet to plan your editorial calendar

- Start with a strategy - make sure the strategy can:

    - first and foremost, lead to the sale of your product or service

    - content that adds value to the lives of your customer

    - content that makes you a thought leader in your field

    - content that has "legs," meaning it will be easy to come up with topics to support the strategy

- Determine your content frequency - how often do you want to post a blog post, post on Facebook, Tweet, etc.? There are a number of theories on what the right frequency is but ultimately it depends on what you have to say and how many people are listening. As the followers start to grow, use really strong content at least once a day on each channel and make sure the content is matched to the channel it is going out to. Don't blanket send the same content across all the channels. Twitter has a short lifecycle whilst Facebook and Blogs can be extended with ease.

- Start filling out your calendar. Make sure to adjust for seasonality, holidays or other events going on in your business

PRO TIP:
Once you get proficient about scheduling your content, use the tools listed above to try some basic automation. Also, pay attention to your data for clues on dates and times that your audience is most receptive to your content.

61

THE CLOSED CAPTION HACK

How to use video text
transcription to excel at SEO

THE PHASE:
Launch

DIFFICULTY:
Intermediate

WE USE:
Several
transcription
services available
(Google It!) or do
it yourself.

The Hack: Using video for SEO is becoming very effective, as Google has begun to give video results higher placement on their search engine results page. Search engines use "rich snippets" to determine what's inside a video, and YouTube specifically uses your title and description to create these rich snippets. The problem is your video contains many more words than these snippets, and those words aren't being indexed. Simple fix - Transcribe your videos for added SEO juice.

Now Hack It:

- Use an online transcription service to transcribe your video's script.

- Once you have the script, include the script on the page or post that includes your video.

- Not only will this allow Google to index all the keywords, it also provides content for customers that prefer reading over watching, as well as hearing impaired customers.

PRO TIP:
As you start to collect transcripts of your videos, consider repurposing the content into other formats, particularly long form. A transcription of a speech or conference presentation can easily create a long-form whitepaper or blog post! Recycle and Reuse, now that's using your head.

62

THE INFOGRAPHIC HACK

How to create engaging infographics for shareable content and SEO backlinks

THE PHASE:
Launch

DIFFICULTY:
Intermediate

WE USE:
Listing site:
http://graphs.
net/100-websites-
to-submit-market-
your-infographic-
for-free.html

The Hack: Infographics are great, everyone loves them. So as marketers we should be creating them. They are consistently amongst the most shared content by bloggers and media sites alike. The more they are shared, the more organic traffic you will attract. As an added benefit, all of those links to your infographic will help you achieve your SEO goals. Double score.

Now Hack It:

- Brainstorm a list of industry topics that would make great infographics:
  - Think of topics that are current and interesting to your customers
  - Research competitors for topics they've used and make sure that you're not about to do what has been done. Also - don't copy what they've done. Be original.
- Use Google image search to determine if the infographic would be unique, this just helps confirm what you've found out from your competitors and will also highlight areas you may not have looked at yet.
  - Think about topics that are data heavy - The more you have to work with, the easier the task will be.
- Use some of the graphic design hacks in this book to get your infographic created. Fiverr, 99designs and Canva can produce great looking infographics cost effectively.
- Once created, share them on your website, social media accounts and blog.
- Now using the list above, submit your infographic to over 100 infographic listing sites in order to leverage them for free traffic and valuable SEO inbound links.

PRO TIP:
If you have more budget to spend on your infographic, definitely use an ad agency or a company like killerinfographics.com to create your content. The better the infographic looks (and the easier the information is presented) the better chance it has of going viral. Ultimately, that is what it is all about.

63

THE VIRAL REFERRAL HACK

How to create a simple and effective viral referral email

THE PHASE:
Launch

DIFFICULTY:
Intermediate

WE USE:
ShareLinkGenerator.com(free) and
MailChimp.com

The Hack: One of our favorite growth hacker Jedi's to follow and learn from is Justin Mares. Not only is he the co-author of the aforementioned "Traction" book, he also offers an amazing email course called Programming for Marketers, which teaches us how to become more technical. One of his hacks creates an elegant viral referral email, yes such things do exist. Not only is it a great idea, Justin was able to implement it into the promotion of his course and had 33% of the audience refer a friend to get bonus content! This one's for you Justin!, you clever Jedi you. The force is definitely strong with this one.

Now Hack It:

- Sidebar Counselor: If you prefer to run this program on social media instead of email, refer to the Pay With a Tweet hack for ideas.

- **Step 1** - Think of an exciting bonus. This is what the referrer will be rewarded with if they complete the referral action. This can be a video, a graphic, a chapter, a white paper, a tool or anything else your customer would want. The better the bonus, the more shares you'll get.

- **Step 2** - Set up your bonus. The easiest way is to create a public folder on Google Drive or Dropbox and copy the public link to the bonus.

- **Step 3** - Create your two referral emails. The first one asks the referrer to share the information by offering the bonus for doing so. The second is the shorter message that will be sent from the referrer to the new potential customer.

- **Step 4** - Take the second email and populate an email share link on sharelinkgenerator.com. Leave the "to" field blank but make sure to populate the "bcc" field with a dedicated customer service email address that you have access to.

- **Step 5** - Add your new share link to the first email that gets sent to referrers. When they click the share link, the email you drafted will be auto-populated, and will bcc your email when sent. Keeping track - just like that!

- **Step 6** - In your email software, setup an auto-responder on that dedicated email address to fulfill the bonus. Simply paste the public Dropbox link from step 2 into the email, so referrers can simply click the link to download the bonus.

PRO TIP:
If you monitor both the number of invites per customer and the conversion rate per invite, you can calculate your K Factor, which is a measure of virality. Simply multiply the number of invites per referrer by the conversion rate of the email. If your K is above 1, you have created a successful referral program that you can grow from. If not, you can either optimize for better success or abort.

64

THE SAMUEL L JACKSON HACK

How to create email messaging that your customers will care about

THE PHASE:
Launch

DIFFICULTY:
Intermediate

WE USE:
Email software

The Hack: "Everybody knows, when you make an assumption, you make an ass out of you and umption." That's Samuel L Jackson dishing out some street wisdom in the movie The Long Kiss Goodnight. Now how does this quote relate to getting users to share your emails? Well, the problem with a lot of what we do in marketing rests on the fact that we make assumptions that may not necessarily be true. This especially applies to growth hacking. It's your job to push the marketing envelope further, which can't be done without assuming certain things about users. One of the most dangerous assumptions made by growth hackers is that their emails are so awesome that users will go out of their way to share them with friends. Wrong! But we're all human. It's time you got introduced to the Samuel L Jackson Email Hack.

Now Hack It:

- Everyone is lazy by nature. Any additional steps that need to be taken or hoops to be jumped through will activate the lazy gene in your app's users. Straight away. Guaranteed. Guess that that means for your emails?

- That's right, you're lucky to have them read, let alone shared. However, you can hack this by creating pre-made "Forward to a Friend" emails following this process:
  - Write your referral email copy, including the CTA.
  - Include a link to your offer landing page in the body.
  - Dump it into Mlto.tk to create a pre-populated email.
  - Add hyperlinks to relevant parts of the message.
  - Wham-bam-thank-you-ma'am. You're done!

- So as Mr. Jackson so eloquently put it, don't make an ass of yourself by assuming that users will forward your emails.

- There, you've just simplified life for your user. In return, their "thank-you's" in the form of invites will increase your referral rates.

65

THE 'SAY NO TO STOCK PHOTOS' HACK

How to use FlashStock to create your own stunning photos

THE PHASE:
Scale

DIFFICULTY:
Intermediate

WE USE:
FlashStock.com

The Hack: At some point, your brand is going to outgrow even the best stock images out there. This realization may come in many forms: you may hit an efficiency ceiling on your social media ads that you can't break through. You might have difficulty telling your brand's story limited by the availability of stock photos. Or worse, you may see other companies using the SAME stock image as you, which is a credibility killer if we've ever seen one (no one likes non-authentic brands!)

So what do you do? Maybe you can take your own or hire a photographer, or hire an advertising agency. All of these have pros and cons, mainly trade-offs between cost and quality. Trade off no more. FlashStock is an Instagram partner company that leverages their global network of photographers to create cost effective photos for you to own exclusively. They have clients as big as Mercedes-Benz and Anheuser Busch, but will also like working with smaller brands.

Here's how:

Now Hack It:

- Visit flashstock.com and fill out a contact form to get the ball rolling.

- The folks at FlashStock will walk you through a creative brief that describes the photos you want to receive.

- You'll be able to provide guidance on the type of people, the settings, the wardrobe, the use of your products and every little detail to ensure your photos are exactly how you want them.

- The brief will go out to the photographers and they will send your finished photos back in a few weeks' time.

- Replace all those ugly stock photos on Facebook and display with your new custom images. Start telling your brand story and engaging your audience in a meaningful way

PRO TIP:
When designing the creative brief, give a lot of thought to the overall strategy and theme – if you can create a theme that has "legs," you can use FlashStock as your image source for years to come. Also, consider showing your photos off by advertising on Instagram and other photo-first social media sites.

66

THE AUSTIN POWERS HACK

How to add a bit of
mystery to your product

THE PHASE:
Launch

DIFFICULTY:
Intermediate

WE USE:
Our imaginations

The Hack: Mystery. No, not the Austin Powers kind. We all know there's only one International Man of Mystery and he don't come cheap. Maybe when you hit that $1 billion IPO… But then you'll be too busy partying to do any growth hacking. Perhaps, even partying with Mr. Powers himself. Groovy.

Anyway, let's get back to the topic at hand.

Mystery. The kind that makes you sit up and pay attention. The kind that leaves Easter eggs in our apps. What? No, not the chocolate variety you gorge yourself on over Easter break.

You knew that apps have hidden features, didn't you? That kind of Easter egg.

Perhaps, this is a hangover that grey-haired developers have nursed all the way from the days of Atari's Adventure or the younger nerd generation have carried into their programming jobs from holding too many Halo all-nighters. It's a well-known fact that many start-ups have added hidden features into their products.

Why are Easter eggs a good growth hack? Because they are unexpected. They rattle our social media-numbed brain-cages, and our brains like a good shake once in a while. So, why not surprise and delight your users into activating their subscription? It just takes a bit of imagination.

Now Hack It:

- Ready, set… Now unleash the full power of your creativity.

- Straight after, tell your developer to implement your genius idea.

- Word of warning: it's probably not safe to let your dev unleash HIS imagination as you may end up with some Star Wars or Dungeons and Dragons-related "surprise." Sorry, devs…

- Don't believe us? Type "use the force Luke" into YouTube's search bar.

- For inspiration, check out these entertaining start-up Easter eggs (fortunately, they're not all Star Wars-related):

  - YouTube's Snake game – press left and up keys on your keyboard when a video is playing.

  - Wistia's Dancing Employees – when on their "About Us" page type "dance" on your keyboard.

  - Google's Barrel Roll – type in "do a barrel roll" into the search field.

  - Firefox's "About" Feature – type in "about:robots" into the search bar.

  - Snapchat's Secret Filters – just read this Buzzfeed guide.

- Now that your creative juices are flowing think of how you can send your users on an Easter egg hunt. They'll love you for it!

67

THE FREE
T-SHIRT HACK

How to give away t-shirts without it becoming a full time job

THE PHASE:
Launch

DIFFICULTY:
Beginner

WE USE:
StartupThreads.
com

The Hack: Have you ever tried to produce t-shirts or other swag for your company - FYI This is a thankless task, only to quickly become overwhelmed by the avalanche of inventory, boxes, packing materials and labels? Truth be told, it almost makes it not worth doing! A kickass company called Startup Threads fixes that problem by handling the entire process - from design and production to fulfillment and shipping to your customers, Startup Threads is a one-stop shop. Genius!

Now Hack It:

- Create an account at startupthreads.com - Select the item(s) you want to offer your customer.

- Their easy to use form allows you to get a customized price based on your selected item, the quantity you need and the number of print colors on the front.

- Upload your artwork and create a design for your swag.

- Now you have this awesome dashboard populated, where you can control who receives your t-shirts. Upload customer lists, select which ones are getting the swag, and presto - Startup Threads will pick and pack the order and ship it to your customer. You never have to touch a mailing label or packing slip!

PRO TIP:
For those of you automation junkies, Startup Threads has an API that allows you to integrate your other marketing systems and automate the fulfillment of t-shirts! Life just got real easy.

68

THE CORPORATE ESPIONAGE HACK

How to spy on your competitors

THE PHASE:
Launch

DIFFICULTY:
Intermediate

WE USE:
iSpionage.com
(30 days free,
then $49/month)

BuzzSumo.com
(free trial, then
$99/month)

CROMonitor.
com (monitors 2
websites for free)

The Hack: Marketing is war. And all is fair in love and war. So all is fair in marketing. Make sense? Good. Keeping track of your competition is really important, don't underestimate this, getting a sneak attack from a competitor is never fun. Not only will you get ideas from their marketing efforts, you'll be able to identify channels that they are NOT using. Here are a few tools that make it easy to keep tabs on your opponents. Attack!

Now Hack It:

- First let's get a general overview of your competitor's marketing plan. Create an account at iSpionage.com and start monitoring your competitor. What you learn will include:

    - their advertising plan and channels

    - their AdWords strategy, budget, keywords and top ads

    - their SEO performance

    - their monthly traffic

    - the same data for their competitors

- Next we're going to spy on their content marketing plan. Head over to buzzsumo.com, create an account and start spying. Here we'll learn:

    - their content marketing plan

    - their top performing content topics

    - their inbound link quality, quantity and leads

    - the influencers who've covered them

    - the amount of social sharing their topics generate

- Lastly we're going to get very sneaky and find out what aspects of their website they're currently testing. We can find out what A/B tests and multivariate tests they are conducting. This gives you extremely valuable insight on the funnel stages they are focused on optimizing, as well as ideas for your own tests.

PRO TIP:
Set up simple Google keyword alerts for all your competitors. Google will send you a daily digest of all the news items on your opponents. Follow-up with journalists that write about your competitors and provide a new angle or topic.

You've now graduated to Super Spy! Well done Mr. Bond.

69

THE CUSTOMER SATISFACTION HACK

How to ensure your customers are happy with one simple question

THE PHASE:
Launch

DIFFICULTY:
Intermediate

WE USE:
Promoter.io
(FREE for 1000
surveys/month)

The Hack: Ah, the Net Promoter Score (NPS) a.k.a. "The Ultimate Question 2.0." A real marketing research institution (as far as digital marketing goes, anyway). The system was developed over a decade ago and has been the metric du jour of corporate marketing departments ever since. Its sole purpose is to measure customer loyalty. Yes, things are different in the growth hacking world that we inhabit. Instead of worrying about such nonsense as NPS, we're obsessing over DAU, WAU, MAU, LTV and other TLAs that make the brain hurt a little for the uninitiated. But, the NPS is not as old-school as you may think.

In fact, other tech start-ups have found it very useful. So, wipe that holier-than-thou snicker off your face because you may learn something new about your users. The real issue of implementing NPS for a start-up is actually the cost of implementing it. For instance, Promoter.io charges $49 for a month for asking one question. Surely, there must be a way to hack this? You betcha! Read on to find out how, our fellow hacker.

Now Hack It:

- The mechanics of an NPS survey are pretty straightforward. A customer is asked the following question:
    - "How likely is it that you would recommend our company/product/service to a friend?"
- They are then asked to provide a rating on a 10-point scale that ranges from "Not at all likely" to "Extremely likely."
- That's it - that is the NPS. That looks like something that should be open-source and free, right?
- But of course, there is a way to hack it and avoid further taxing your already-overtaxed MarTec stack budget.
- There are two things you need to do first:
    - Register for a basic plan with Wufoo.
    - Download an NPS survey template from Sendwithus.com.
- Follow the instructions on how to get Wufoo and Sendwithus to work harmoniously together and start saving some serious coin.
- All the while, your users will keep you informed on what they think of your product.
- A true win-win.

70
THE TRANSLATION HACK

How to painlessly translate your
website into multiple languages

THE PHASE:
Launch and
Optimize

DIFFICULTY:
Advanced

WE USE:
Duolingo

The Hack: The World Wide Web is a big place. The English speaking
portion of it accounts for only 55% off all of the content on the
internet. By performing a very simple calculation, it becomes obvious
that your SaaS app is missing out on a whopping 45% percent of
the world's non-English speaking population. But what to do?

Get creative, that's what! One of the lesser-known hacks that
Facebook did was to build an entire stand-alone app that allowed
users to translate the website into their language of choice. A more
recent example is BuzzFeed who partnered up with language-
teaching app Duolingo. The hack involves getting Duolingo's app
users to translate English phrases into their native language as part
of their language training program.

While these hacks aren't as easily replicable as your vanilla growth
hacks, the thinking behind them should inspire you to start looking at
news ways of scaling your application.

Now Hack It:

- There is actually no ready-made hack for this so you'll have to activate your brain cells to pull this one off.

- Share whatever you come up with and we'll be happy to feature you in the sourcebook!

CASE STUDY #7
MATT EPSTEIN
VP OF
MARKETING,
ZENEFITS

Set your goal, then double it

Founded in May 2013, Zenefits is considered to be the fastest growing SaaS company. Today, it has achieved Unicorn status with a valuation of over $4.5 billion and over 1,200 employees. Despite its astronomical growth, Zenefits had humble beginnings, starting out the "old school" way in the CEO and Co-Founder's kitchen. In those days, the company was a team of three, with founders Parker Conrad and Laks Srini hiring their first employee Matt Epstein, now VP of Marketing.

Zenefits first originated from Parker's own frustration with the constant headaches that came along with running a business - managing payroll, health insurance, compliance, onboarding, offboarding. It might not stop you from running a business, but it does eat precious hours out of your work week. At the time, there were plenty of companies that offered tools to help companies manage HR, but Zenefits' objective was to eliminate all the noise and keep things simple by creating an "apple-esque" design that was more user-friendly, and a product so effective, it does the thinking for you. In a nutshell, Zenefits wants to make it effortless for you to run your business.

For the past three years, Zenefits has been consistently setting and surpassing its traction goals. The target was getting a strong hockey stick effect, a key indicator investors look for. The hockey stick effect is when your growth curve (or whatever KPI you're tracking, revenue, visits, users) begins at a normal linear pace and then takes off at an exponential rate.

In the beginning, the team focused on customers, not revenue. The initial traction goal was to gain 30 customers in three months. The significance being it's much easier at the start to focus on customers over revenue metrics. Once Zenefits had hit product-market fit, Parker set the target for the team to achieve two million in revenue in a year. Going from almost zero to two million in revenue is no small feat. The following year, Parker had his "Steve Jobs Moment" and set the revenue milestone to $10 million, only to change his mind the day after and demand $20 million instead. The 10X'd revenue goal seemed absolutely impossible to Matt, however this outrageous mission forced him and his marketing team to think in ways they had never thought possible.

With a clear set game plan, here is how Matt and his team achieved $20 million in revenue in a single year:

Find your secret sauce

Your secret sauce, as Matt describes it, is composed of three things: your messaging, your audience and where you get your lead sources from. The easiest way to determine this is email marketing. Originally, Matt simply emailed people in his and Parker's network. He AB tested 100 emails every day for two months by sending out two different versions. Focusing on emails allowed him to hone in on the right messaging that attracted the most customers. With AB testing email, it's important to craft the general message in three sentences or less in a way that will grab people's attention. Then there are the nuances within those three sentences, if you remove or change one word or add a certain phrase, does it get a better result. Matt recommends to start the morning by coming up with two new ways of packaging and selling the product, and AB test them. Send the emails out to as many people as possible. Through this tactic, Matt learned that HR professionals were not his actual target market, but rather C-level executives were much more receptive. Once he learned this, he was able to understand how to generate the most effective messaging towards this new found target market. When the growth target shifted from two to $20 million in revenue, Matt simply scaled email. They began doing a lot of email distribution through partners, a lot of opt-ins and using a lot of different landing pages. However, without the time invested at the start, they could not have effectively scaled email to actually be a viable channel.

Use Lightweight CRM to Scale Sales

A common mistake many companies make when it comes to sales is either they don't implement Customer Relationship Management software or they immediately get on SalesForce. You're either not collecting data, or you're using a very complex system that requires a lot of training to maximize the software. Matt began hiring Sales Development Reps and to help them scale they implemented a lightweight CRM for the first year. The benefit of doing this according to Matt was, "we knew exactly what our process was, exactly what our pipeline looked like, exactly what information we captured and so when we made the transition to SalesForce it only took a few weeks to get implemented, and that's when we started really scaling." When asked which lightweight CRM he recommended, Matt suggested Close.io, however he could not stress enough for them a B2B SaaS company, SalesForce is the bedrock of your business. If it is not set up properly, your automation on the marketing campaigns and metrics will be incorrect. The beautiful thing about SDRs according to Matt is, "that you can expect X amount of opportunities per month." According to him, a good baseline for success with SDRs are around 35 sales qualified leads a month, 18-30 opportunities, and you want about 60 per cent to 75 per cent from demo to opportunity. Simply put, a qualified lead is someone who meets your qualifications and an opportunity is when there is an realistic chance it will close. To scale sales to meet Parker's ambitious goals, Matt simply grew the team from a couple of SDR's to 40, now Zenefits has over 400.

Pull Every Lever

As Zenefits growth began to enter hyper-mode, the team could no longer rely on email and SDR's to scale the company. At this stage every bit counts, testing PPC, Display Ads and Radio. According to Matt, "the whole thing is to test as many things as possible as fast as possible. As soon as you see a flicker of life, throw fire on it until it breaks." Native advertisements were one of the channels that the team focused on once they noticed some positive early results. One of the creative tactics they used was with PPC. They targeted prospects who were in their tracking pixel and would fill up every ad space on the person's browser and a bus would drive across the screen saying "rolling out the future of HR." For those who don't know tracking pixels, they are a tiny image that allows you to keep track of people who either visited your website or saw your advertisement. This tactic was a powerful way for the team to stay target potential prospects and continue to engage them through multiple touch points.

Zenefits has proven to be one of the most successful B2B SaaS companies to date, far exceeding expectations. As the company transitioned through the different growth phases, it continued to set and exceed its ambitious goals. From 30 customers in three months, to over two million in revenue the following year and reaching over twenty million in revenue the year after. Zenefits sights are now set on $100 million in revenue.

So what would Matt like marketers to learn from Zenefits experience?

Firstly, make your stretch goal the actual goal. One of the strategies both Parker and Matt have stressed is the importance of setting stretch goals as your actual goals. The reason is that the stretch goal is normally ignored and people tend to settle for hitting slightly above or below the primary goal. As Matt explains, "if your goal is one million in revenue and your stretch goal is five million in revenue, if you hit one million you will be satisfied with hitting that goal. But if you set a five million revenue goal, even if you fall way short and only hit three million, it is still far better than the million dollar goal." Setting these monstrous goals will force you to think outside the box.

Secondly, don't let your limitations limit you. Often people are hesitant to scale a growth channel even when it is very successful. When Matt asks people why they haven't tried to 10X a channel that is successful, they never seem to have a good answer. In most cases Matt explains, "people don't scale up because they are nervous and scared, the big number scares them." Really successful leaders, when something works they put their foot on the pedal and worry about crashing later.

Finally, begin and end the conversation in data. According to Matt, "the biggest mistake I made was listening to my team. You should never listen to each other. The only thing you should listen to is data." While this statement was a little tongue and cheek, the lesson is critical, use data to drive decisions. Data will often times tell a different story than what people tend to think or assume. Remember, we are all guilty of certain biases, with data you can mitigate against those issues.

SCALING FOR GROWTH

Hopefully by this point you've mastered Product/Market Fit and you used the hacks in the Transitioning to Growth section to find some channels that promised efficient customer acquisitions.

Congratulations growth hackers! The odds were against you and I'm sure you battled through some big challenges to get here.

Now to burst your bubble: The book Traction introduced a (hilarious) law called "The Law of Shitty

Click-Throughs" which posited that every acquisition channel will eventually become inefficient as more and more competitors enter the channel and drive up the costs.

The good news is that every emerging channel presents a window of opportunity (that can be weeks, months or years) in which you will be able to efficiently acquire customers during that time period. So they're totally worth looking for – you just have to be on the lookout for the plateau and/or the decline in your marketing efficiency.

Now that you have identified some high potential, high ceiling channels, you want to milk them for all they're worth. That will involve inter-channel experimentation, A/B testing, testing your creative and messaging, testing different ad units and getting the funnel as HOT as possible.

Just like we moved up the funnel in the last section, we will want to endeavor even further up the funnel, right to the top! Since we need more leads to move our new needle, we need to focus on mass marketing (and more risky) channels that can support the scale of growth that the business will need. Smart growth marketers - even when faced with inherently less track-able channels - will leverage the tracking tools they've built previously to get a good idea for what mass channels are working, there by reducing the risk of these channels.

Brand awareness becomes a key focus, and loading as many leads into the top of the funnel leads to accelerated profit growth. As the top of the funnel velocity increases, you'll want to optimize to remove all slack and friction from the funnel. You'll also want to make sure that you have the right team in place, experienced in and capable of achieving this rapid growth.

All the pieces of the startup marketing puzzle start to fall in to place. As explained by Tomasz

Tunguz "In this way, a startup can match the growth needs and the predictability needs of each type of marketing channel with the needs of the startup, namely the ability to grow and also demonstrate compelling unit economics and repeatable growth, the cornerstone of successful fundraising".

That's what I'm talking about! Let's do this!

71

THE SERIOUS SEO HACK

How to use Moz to get serious about your SEO

THE PHASE:
Scale

DIFFICULTY:
Advanced

WE USE:
Moz.com (30 days free, $99/month for standard membership)

The Hack: You've probably spent much of your marketing time and $$'s focusing on paid advertising channels that can be optimized to drive traffic to your site profitably. And that's a great thing to be focused on because you want to establish scalable, predictable and repeatable marketing channels, and paid is the fastest way to do so.

But at some point you're going to want scale back your paid traffic in favor of free organic traffic. Everybody loves doing and getting stuff for free. To do so, you're going to have to get more advanced and aggressive with your analytics and SEO data and focus more resources on organic traffic. Because really, the company that gets the most free traffic is going to be tough to beat (and we want that to be us!)

Moz is a longtime leader in the SEO space, led by their CEO Rand Fishkin, who's widely considered the Yoda of SEO. This is a great tool for when you're ready to get serious about SEO.

Now Hack It:

- Sign up for an account at Moz.com. You have to enter credit card information, but you won't be charged in the first 30 days.

- Begin with a site audit so you can establish a baseline for your performance.

- Enter information on your direct competitors so you can benchmark your performance against theirs.

- Let Moz's analytics provide you with insights to get quick SEO wins for your site.

PRO TIP:
Like all experiments with data, it can be overwhelming to marketers who are not strong with analytics. The key is to start slow. Pick two or three key metrics and follow them compulsively, but not so compulsively that you dream about it at night! Pay attention to how your day-to-day levers impact your key performance indicators.

72

THE ANTI-BAIT-AND-SWITCH HACK

How to match your offer to your page content

THE PHASE:
Scale

DIFFICULTY:
Intermediate

WE USE:
SumoMe or Hello
Bar (free
trials available)

After spending a considerable amount of time developing your blog, the virtual blood, sweat and tears have paid off. You now have a number posts on your blog that drive a considerable amount of traffic to your site. The flipside of this is that they may not be the highest-converting pages. Once a visitor has landed on your page, they typically don't have any incentive to stick around and move on to the next thing that catches their fancy. Usually, the "next thing" is not on your website.

But this is something that you can - and should - take care of. As a growth hacker, you need to maximize the return on your content assets by turning as many of your visitors into subscribers or leads. Think of this hack as being the anti-"bait and switch."

Now Hack It:

- Undertake a "bounce rate stock take" using Google Analytics to identify pages with excessively high percentages.

- Find an incentive that you could provide to visitors of each of those pages, such as a free eBook, whitepaper, report or other relevant content resource.

- The important thing here is to make sure that the incentive matches up with the content in your post. This shouldn't be too hard to figure out as your blog topic will suggest the freebie.

- If you want to get even more "jiggy with it," you can try and match the content freebie to the stage of the buyer journey that a visitor of the page could be at. Doing so would significantly increase the perceived value of your incentive.

- The way to implement this is to use Hello Bar or any one of the numerous opt-in form pop-up plugins. You can always A/B test these to see what works best.

- As always, don't forget to keep track of the relevant statistics afterwards.

73

THE ENCLOSED CHECKOUT HACK

How to match your offer to your page content

THE PHASE:
Scale

DIFFICULTY:
Intermediate

WE USE:
Olark

You see it time and again in your ecommerce analytics reports: the user happily bounces through your funnel without so much as a cloud of doubt on their way to the checkout horizon. Then once they get to your shopping cart. Boom - they're gone! Cart abandoned. What just happened?

Checkout abandonment is a b... bad deal. And common. All too common. In fact, the lowest percentage of online shopping cart abandonment rates is estimated at 69.1%. That is pretty high for what is meant to be the "lower" percentage! Let's now explore how your shopping cart can avoid becoming yet another ecommerce statistic.

The answer: "enclosed checkout process." That is what will make all the difference to your conversion rates and activations. And this growth hack doesn't just apply to ecommerce businesses but to your SaaS app also. You do have a checkout process, don't you?

Now Hack It:

- Take all of those fancy menus and buttons in your nav pane. Now "strip" them out as if you were turning an old rust bucket into a hot rod.

- Because that's what you're doing. You're transforming your ol' clunker of a shopping cart into the equivalent of a show-stopping street machine.

- So, take out all of the necessary nav elements and just leave your company logo. This becomes the ONLY means of escape now. Does this remind you of anything?

- If you answered "landing page" then this reward sticker is for you! Because this is what your cart is now, the most lucrative kind of landing page.

- Definitely keep all of the important links: delivery options, returns policy, contacts details and the necessary legalese. BUT turn them into lightbox pop-ups or overlays rather than links that take the user off the page.

- Allow users to navigate back and forth through the checkout process in case they need to change any information. This is so that they're not forced to click the browser's "back" button.

- NEVER let your users click the back button...

- You can also experiment with including a "live chat" option such as Zopim or Olark9.

- 69% abandonment rate? Pfft, not with this bad boy that you've just built.

74

THE EXIT INTENT HACK

How to convert bouncers into customers

THE PHASE:
Scale

DIFFICULTY:
Advanced

WE USE:
Ouibounce

Exit intent apps are The Bizness for increasing your on-page conversions. Caught a user navigating away from the checkout mid-way through their order?

Bam! Special offer pop-up.

See a visitor sneaking their way towards the "Back" button while reading your blog.

Bam! Email subscription opt-in form.

Notice a slowly cursor inching towards the browser's address bar while browsing your home page?

Bam... Bam... Bam!

Yes, this must be conversion heaven...The only thing that isn't really awesome about apps like Bounce-Exchange and their ilk is the price. As in, it's not inspiring at all. Can your bootstrapped start-up really afford to spend a minimum of $3,995 per month on an exit intent popup app? C'mon! And, yes, there are now cheaper alternatives. However, there are a couple that we would like to bring to your attention due to their growth hacker-friendly price: free. Growth Hacker, meet your new on-page conversion marketing sidekick.

Now Hack It:

- There are two notable open-source alternatives:

  - The cute-sounding Ouibounce.

  - And the very meat-and-potatoes alternative, Exit-intent plugin. Hey, nothing wrong with having an app that clearly says what it does and then does what it says. If only more apps were as clear about their purpose in life...

- Both solutions require a bit of coding to get them up and running. The payoff is that, once deployed on your website, they won't cost you a cent to run.

- Now just think about it, even your monthly intake of coffee costs a magnitude more than something that will help you to convert users by the hundreds or thousands.

- Now THAT deserves a celebratory $5 latte!

75

THE TWITTER NINJA HACK

How to massively grow your Twitter follower count

THE PHASE:
Scale

DIFFICULTY:
Beginner

WE USE:
Tweepi.com (free accounts exist but the $14.99/month plan is most user friendly and powerful)

This hack is one of the hackiest hacks in the book. The reason being it's technical, it's experimentational and it requires you to look at a channel in a different way.

When growing your Twitter followers with an automation tool, you need to think of your followers not as individual leads but more like seeds being planted in soil. The reason is that you are going to use a high velocity of following and unfollowing twitter accounts in order to grow your following.

While this seems counter-intuitive at the beginning (old school thinking: Hey! All these accounts are potential customers who need to be loved and nurtured), the process is the fastest way we've used to grow Twitter accounts to over 5k followers.

Now Hack It:

- Sign up at Tweepi.com. Tweepi can be confusing to register to because you need a username and a linked Twitter account. The easiest way to register is to sign up with your Twitter account.

- Make sure your account is looking good. Have a great photo, header photo, bio and links, so your profile looks as appealing as possible.Canva.com has templates for Twitter headers.

- Twitter's rules on how many people you can follow are strict, so there's a game to high velocity follower growth. You can follow up to 2000 people, but you can't break that barrier until 1500 people follow you. Then you can increase above 2000 at a similar ratio to your own followers.

- Start following people based on any number of search parameters. You can follow competitors friends and followers (often the easiest wins), non-competitive accounts, influencer accounts or association accounts. Start following people but don't go too fast. Pay attention to Tweepi's rules on how many people to follow.

- Wait a period of time to see how many of these accounts follow you back. You decide what's an appropriate amount of time, but 2-3 days is standard.

- After your defined amount of time, filter users who aren't following you back and start unfollowing them. Once completed, start following more people based on existing or new search parameters.

- Every new follow batch is an experiment so keep track of the data on a spreadsheet. Fields such as date, role model account, followers or friends, how many you followed, how many were left to follow, and what percent followed you back.

PRO TIP:
If you track your data carefully, you'll notice certain segments following you back at a higher rate than the rest (i.e., - competitors, bloggers, etc.).Use that knowledge to better target your follows on the next experiments.

76

THE ORBTR HACK

How to make your website content personal

THE PHASE:
Scale

DIFFICULTY:
Intermediate

WE USE:
Orbtr

The Hack: Context marketing. It's the as-yet-unexplored frontier of digital marketing. But wait, wait, waaait... Context? Marketing? Before you get all Sherlock Holmes on us and leave this page to explore the netherworlds of Google, we'll clarify what we mean.

For our purposes, context marketing refers to personalizing a website's content based on the visitor's previous history of interacting with your start-up. Not just your website, not just your email drip campaign, not just your paid advertising but ANY and ALL of these channels. It is no mean feat to achieve true context personalization and would usually require an expensive marketing automation suite such as Hubspot with their Content Optimization System. However, this awesome app makes it possible to carry out context marketing even on your Ramen budget

Now Hack It:

- Just so we're all on the same page, let's give an example of how context marketing works:

- A new visitor, who has never been to your website before, lands on your home page.

- However, after downloading a white paper and submitting their details via a form page and sees the same generic message that every other first-time visitor would see, that same visitor sees their name on returning to your site. Creepy? Only if you make it so it actually makes a lot of sense.

- Sounds cool, right? But Hubspot's COS system may be beyond your reach at this stage.

- Well, ORBTR and its contextual marketing widget may just be the answer. In addition to dynamic content, this full-blown marketing automation suite can integrates with most of the apps in your current growth hacking toolkit.

- Here's how to actually contextualize your website:

  - Place a code snippet in strategically chosen parts of your Wordpress site.

  - Configure your "Orbits" to trigger different messages depending on your user's actions.

- With such personalization, your users won't have a choice but to be over the moon about using your app.

- To top it off, this amazing piece of tech only costs $99 per month!

- After your defined amount of time, filter users who aren't following you back and start unfollowing them. Once completed, start following more people based on existing or new search parameters.

- Every new follow batch is an experiment so keep track of the data on a spreadsheet. Fields such as date, role model account, followers or friends, how many you followed, how many were left to follow, and what percent followed you back.

77

THE DEAL MAKER HACK

How to hustle your way to big partnerships

THE PHASE:
Scale

DIFFICULTY:
Intermediate

WE USE:
Our Hustle

The Hack: You scratch my back, I'll scratch yours. This business tenet has been fundamental to the growth of companies long before The Internet was even so much as a twinkle in Tim Berners-Lee's eyes.

Even tech start-ups have been using partnerships ever since Microsoft started bribing PC manufacturers into bundling their operating system with every new computer shipped. So, what's different for SaaS start-ups? In one word: nothing. What worked hundreds of years ago still works today. That's the good news! However, as a growth hacker, this territory may be more foreign to you given the virtual nature of most of the BizDev activity you're used to. That's OK, we'll gently guide you through this strange land where suits are worn daily and cigars are still smoked. You better believe it...

Now Hack It:

- A little skeptical that old-school business tactics can help you growth hack your way to glory in today's API-driven world?

- In that case, Uber is a fantastic example of how a modern tech start-up has strategically used partnerships to grow at a phenomenal rate.

- Partnerships are actually not as daunting as the thick stack of legal paperwork that comes standard with them

- Sure, they involve a lot more people interaction than you may be used to but growth hacking is growth hacking, whether it's offline or online.

- Here's what you can do to sell the value of a strategic partnership to another start-up:

- Sell the benefits of partnering with your start-up and how your product can add value to their customers

- Align your vision around a common goal that you both share.

- Carefully think through the logistical and legal aspects of the relationship. Value to the other start-up's business. Yes, this is where it gets boring but just keep the ultimate goal in mind and have good legal advice on hand for when the deal is ready to go through.

- Keep it agile! Start-ups operate in a world that is uncertain by definition so ensure that there is flexibility built into the relationship. This way, when the market moves, your strategic partnership will move with it and continue to make money for both you and your business partner.

- Bring back the three-martini lunch we say!

78

THE 'WHAT GETS MEASURED GETS MANAGED' HACK

How to know which startups metrics are critical to measure

THE PHASE:
Scale

DIFFICULTY:
Intermediate

WE USE:
Excel

You started in the growth hacking game because you get excited by numbers. Crazy numbers, that is. Like growing your users base 6000% in under a year. Or hacking revenue growth to 300% month-on-month. You know, those kind of numbers. As a growth hacker, you never signed up to learn a new language though. MRR.LTV. CMRR.MAU.DAU.CAC. MQL… Blah! Need we go on? Sad but true, metrics are as much a part of the growth hacking game as your gold plated iPhone 6. Oh sorry, are you not one of the co-founders of Facebook? In that case, as much as your desktop drum set.

But you have no choice. A growth hacker lives and dies by the metrics! So, put on your oversized hipster glasses, grab a soy latte and prepare for a session of rote learning. And here you were thinking that growth hacking was all about beating the co-founders at table tennis...

Now Hack It:

- So, let's get down to this metrics business. Out of all of the crazy acronyms that you should be tracking, there is a small list of those that will fill your phone's inbox with smiley face emoticons from your investors.

- That alone is worth the price of filling your brain cavities with more senseless acronyms.

- Without further ado, meet your new best (nerdy) friends:

    - Churn - your arch-nemesis. The one metric you need to beat into submission.

    - CMRR (Contracted Monthly Recurring Revenue) - this mouthful of a metric.

    - Cash - this one needs no introduction. If you ain't got much of this then you are in trouble

    - LPC (Lifetime Profit per Customer) - shows you how much you're really making per customer

    - Customer Acquisition Cost Ratio - you kn ow all that VC money that you've spent to acquire your customers

    - Cost Per Acquisition - you know this one. Oh yeah - you KNOW this one. Until it's as small as a mouse. See customers cancelling? Kung-fu their butts with a discount - that'll do it. For now measures something important. Just don't try to work it out at home - best left to the big-wig growth hackers at places like Amazon need to start hustling making from each sucker, ehm, user over the course of their custom with your shady operation. Pretty useful stuff but a little hard to compute been blowing on 'marketing' over the last few months? Well, this metric will tell you how long it will take to recoup it all. One of the more depressing numbers to look at so don't bother with it on Fridays. It's the one the CEO always tells you to keep under control. But then you go and try that new awesome ad exchange or upload a new custom audience into Facebook. Remember, admitting you have a problem is half the battle

- There... Wipe the sweat of your glasses and get back to reading BuzzFeed. Just the fact that you (sort-of) know what these mean puts you well ahead of the pack.

- Ok, ok. Go and get yourself another soy latte - you deserved it!

79

THE ZAP
HACK

How to make life easier with Zapier

THE PHASE:
Scale

DIFFICULTY:
Intermediate

WE USE:
Zapier.com
(Free for 5 zaps,
plans range from
$20-$75/month)

Give a man a fish and you will feed him for a day. Teach a man to fish and you will feed him for a lifetime or turn him into an industrial tycoon. Supply and demand people!

That's kind of how we feel about Zapier. While debates on their pronunciation are abound (Zap-ee-Er or the more Canadian Zap-ee-eh?), they are a technology company that can be viewed as a payment processor for APIs.

For those who don't know, API's are techspeak for connectors that can hook up one system to another and allow them to communicate with each other in a controlled and secure fashion. What Zapier does is allow you to easily create rules and automations by combining hundreds of company's APIs in one place.

So if you want one system to perform an action based on a trigger from another system, Zapier will let you create those automation rules. We chose not to illustrate a specific example below to underscore that the key learning here is to get comfortable using Zapier and experiment a lot. Knowing the capabilities can save you a lot of time and open up new marketing doors. And trust us when we say, it is one of the easiest tools to setup. Check it out and see if any of the programs you're currently using can be connected together. If so, give it a go. It's free to start with.

Now Hack It:

- Create a free account at Zapier.com.

- Review their list of apps that they integrate with. Spend some time studying the popular zaps, as this is the best way to get ideas for your own automations.

- Creating a zap begins with selecting the two apps you want to integrate and authorizing Zapier to have access to them. Zapier uses a really simple wizard to help guide you through this process.(Authorizing apps usually involves finding the app's API key from their own settings panel. Once you find the key and enter it as requested, it does the work and tests the connections).

- Once authorized, go through the wizard to create your own rule. When complete, test the rule with sample data and make sure the connection is working. Test the rule until you're satisfied that it's working

PRO TIP:
I'll tell you a secret, it's not always as easy as we described, this depends very much on the applications you're trying to get talking to each other. There are limitations. There can be a learning curve when it comes to troubleshooting that takes some time and dedication to overcome. But it's not a technical learning curve, it's more experimentational. Try to automate a bunch of little tasks to get the hang of creating zaps. Challenge: Try to get your Gmail account to send out a pre-populated email every time you update an email address in a Google Drive/Sheets file.

80

THE FORTUNE 500 HACK

How to use LinkedIn to sell into Fortune 500 companies

THE PHASE:
Scale

DIFFICULTY:
Intermediate

WE USE:
Linkedin.com

As Juliana Crispo explained in her awesome blog post entitled "How to Sell In To Any Fortune 500 Company with this LinkedIn Hack" (http://www.saleshacker.com/lead-generation/sell-fortune-500-linkedin-hack/), there's a massive difference between selling into an SMB and selling into a global giant. The direct tactics and entrepreneurial spirit that endears you to SMBs is ignored by Fortune 500 buyers.

When her company Ghostery challenged each member of their sales team by giving them $5,000 to acquire a customer, most of the sales force struggled with various outbound techniques.

Not our Juliana.

While everyone was pushing, she started pulling. Juliana spent her money on LinkedIn ads that drove more inbound leads than she was able to handle. Be like Juliana. Use this hack when you want to snag a very BIG fish.

Now Hack It:

- Create an advertisers account at Linkedin.com. The key to LinkedIn advertising is corporate targeting. Target your top persona very specifically and create a small but buyer rich audience.

- Match your advertising message to the top area of pain that your target buyer is experiencing. Whenever possible, offer them the ability to download a valuable piece of content or have access to a useful tool. A combination of the relevant message and the valuable content offer can be irresistible. Sometimes all it takes is that carrot!

- Drive the ad clicks to a very simple landing page. Ask the lead for the minimal amount of information. Every field you add here will reduce the response rate greatly, so resist. The conversion here is to collect and email and deliver what you promised.

- The content is the new version of your 15 minutes in their office. It's your chance to show them that you understand their needs, and can be trusted. Don't blow it. Bring your A-Game. Invest some time and money into making sure that what you've promised is worth having.

- Nurture the leads. This is where Juliana suggests that the right path is different depending on the situation. But generally walking the lead through a simple buyer intent model will ensure that you deliver the right message at the right time.

PRO TIP:
Constantly measure and constantly optimize. These campaigns rarely work right out of the gate. More often they're the result of data-centric nurturing and a slow but compounding improvement week to week.

CASE STUDY #8
HANA ABAZA
VP MARKETING, UBERFLIP

Selling the Content

Nestled in Liberty Village, a trendy burgeoning neighborhood in Toronto, lies one of Canada's hottest startups, Uberflip. Its main goal is to improve the way companies scale and grow their content marketing operation. In the seven years since its inception, Uberflip has grown from an 'early-stage' startup, to over 1,800 customers and 50 employees. Uberflip gives marketers the necessary tools to publish, evaluate, optimize and promote their content at every stage of the buyer journey, boosting engagement and generating more leads.

Leading the charge of driving growth at Uberflip is Hana Abaza, VP of Marketing. In order to meet the growing needs of the sales team, Hana was tasked with scaling lead generation. In June 2015, her goal was to increase lead generation by 40 per cent, compared to the previous three month average of 3,295. According to Hanna, the key was "to maintain quality and ultimately a steady CAC ratio. We don't want to just pay or overpay for a bunch of leads".

Scaling leads as a B2B SaaS company can be tricky, especially when targeting mid-marketing to large enterprise businesses. To avoid overpaying for leads, Hana needed an approach that would virtually guarantee getting in front of the ideal customer. One of Uberflip's best converting content channels for lead generation has been webinars.

To achieve her ambitious goals, Hana decided to organize Uberflip's first series, "The Marketing Automation Hacks Webinar Series." This strategy targeted one of its key buyer personas, the person that oversees and manages marketing automation at their respective company. The series consisted of six webinars in six days and featured some of the top experts in the following marketing automation platforms: HubSpot, Eloqua, Act-On, Pardot, MailChimp and Marketo. According to Hana, the idea was "to provide excellent content that was 100 per cent aligned with our target customer while giving us a platform to show how Uberflip integrates with each MAP (marketing automation platform) in a relevant context". With a strategy in place and a clear target, here is how Uberflip increased its lead generation by over 40 per cent:

Leverage Partners

Often one of the biggest mistakes companies make with content marketing is doing it completely independently and not leveraging additional external resources. Hana collaborated with partners to help amplify distribution, provide experts and create the content. For example, Hana partnered with MailChimp who provided two experts, Allyson Van Houten a product marketing lead, and Ariana Hargrave head of client relations to run the MailChimp Hacks webinar. To make it easy each partner was provided with the following:

- a one page summary of the series;
- two partner links to track registrants that they send (one to the main landing page with all six webinars, and one to its individual page);
- the option to participate in lead sharing;
- social media messaging and images;
- email copy to help promote its specific webinar to the target audience;
- a co-branded presentation template.

Using this strategy Uberflip was able to secure top experts with Marketo, HubSpot, MailChimp, Pardot, Act-On and Eloqua.

Control Content Structure

This may seem like a no-brainer, but to ensure that each expert's presentation maximized Uberflip and its connection with the MAP, templates were created to determine the structure and flow of each webinar. To keep the structure simple, Hana moderated the webinar. After a brief introduction, the expert had 30-40 minutes to cover marketing automation hacks using the featured platform, followed by a demo showcasing how to use Uberflip with the platform and ended with a Q&A session. According to Hana, the decision to do the Uberflip demo before the Q&A was deliberate, it was important to showcase how Uberflip worked with each MAP. Additionally, this was a strategy to ensure that Uberflip was covered before people began to drop off towards the end. The format was very successful at showcasing Uberflip while also achieving strong attendance throughout the entire session.

Targeted Distribution

For Hana it was important to target a variety of other channels to promote the webinar series. The purpose of this approach was to increase the reach of the series, while still targeting quality leads. Hana focused on several channels that would allow her to target her ideal customer. Starting with people already in the Uberflip email list, two emails were sent, one segmented by which MAP the person used and a second general email about the entire series. One of the ways Uberflip reaches potential customers is through its active blog, this time around a webinar teaser featuring each expert were added. Twitter and LinkedIn have always been effective channels to reach the target customer for Uberflip, with this in mind Hana ran both organic and paid campaigns. Another highly targeted channel Hana took advantage of were the following online communities: LinkedIn groups, user forums and advocate hubs. On top of these experiments, Hana also used paid email placements with authoritative publications in the marketing space. Finally, each expert guest also promoted the webinar through their own channels. These additional channels allowed the Uberflip team to maximize its reach and promote the webinar series to a larger audience and begin targeted lead generation.

Lead Nurture and Sales Team Follow Up

Keeping in mind that the purpose of Hana's strategy was to increase the quality leads, she knew it was important to get the sales team involved early. Rather than waiting until the webinar was over, Uberflip's sales team were included in the process. Sales reps were alerted to leads that had registered for the webinar, who were considered a good fit for Uberflip, and who are engaged with the content. This allowed the sales team to have a conversation with leads before the series even started, resulting in some leads becoming customers. After the webinar series was over, Hana worked with the sales team to craft a quality outreach strategy. This strategy segmented each prospective lead based on which MAP they used and how they can use it with Uberflip to maximize their content marketing efforts.

The marketing automation hacks webinar series successfully surpassed Hana's goal of increasing lead generation by 40 per cent. Monthly leads increased from 3,295 in May to 4,829 in June, an increase of 46 per cent. Additionally, Hana has seen other benefits come from the series, "as time passes, we're able to see the bottom line impact. Since then, we can see that the six days of the MA Hacks Series has generated 45 opportunities for our sales team which translates into approximately half a million in annual pipeline".

Hana had a few key lessons that she felt were important for marketers to take away:

First, know your customers inside and out! It is essential to understand exactly who you are targeting and why. As Hana said, "everything you do should be tightly aligned with who you are doing it for". Understanding your ideal customer is critical if you want to effectively reach them in your marketing efforts.

Second, leverage partners that have a common audience. This is one of the most effective ways to expand your audience and create a win-win with other people in your industry. Only do this when there is an opportunity for each person to benefit. Partnering with another startup when neither company has an audience or any traction just does not make sense. When approaching a person or company to propose a partnership, it is important to make it as easy and enticing as possible for them. It goes without saying that any partnership that you do propose must be mutually beneficial for each party.

Finally, process matters. Creating a clearly defined process to execute on your marketing and growth goals is essential. Many startups avoid doing this based on a misguided belief that structure will be limiting and slow them down, when in fact it is the opposite. The process shouldn't be overly complicated, it does however need to exist in a way that will empower people to use it.

81

THE EMAIL COURSE HACK

How to become a thought leader by offering an email course

THE PHASE:
Scale

DIFFICULTY:
Intermediate

WE USE:
Any email software can automate but GetDrip.com makes it easy

The Hack: Our friend Rob Walling over at Drip does an amazing job of using email courses to engage their potential customers and PROVE to them that they have what the customer needs. What's cool is that their software allows you to easily launch email courses, so not only are you learning why they're a good growth hacking tool, you're seeing it in action!

In fact, we met our publisher (Tom Morkes from Insurgent Publishing) through an email course he launched on self-publishing. By the end of the course, we were convinced that Tom understood our space, was an expert on digital publishing and promotion, and was the right publisher for us.

So yeah, this stuff totally works! Your customer isn't always ready to buy when you're ready to sell. Life would be a lot easier if they were right! Establishing yourself as a thought leader ensures that your brand is top-of-mind when the customer is ready. And it's easy and pretty close to free. What are you waiting for? B2B marketers, we're looking at you!

Now Hack It:

- Brainstorm a topic for your e-course. Make it something your customers are struggling with but always ensure that the topic sells your product. We're not doing this for kicks. And make sure it is something you're confident to teach about.

- Develop an outline consisting of an overview of what they'll learn and then 6-7 emails that teach an issue each.

- Write your emails. Keep them concise, focused and punchy. This is your big chance to prove to a lead that you know their predicament better than they do. This my friend is a form of insight selling.

- Automate them into a drip campaign using your email software. Set them up to go out on your chosen frequency (for example one a day for a week).

- Don't forget to pepper your courses with different calls to action. Some leads will convert early and others may take to the very end.

PRO TIP:
Try to match your content to the buyer stage your customer is in. For example, an early lesson can provide an overview of the problem and the customer's challenges. A later email can talk about solving the product with your solution. A final email may even offer a promotion or a special offer. Just make sure you don't give it up in the first one, remember - no one is going to buy the cow if they get the milk for free.

82

THE REFERRAL SEGMENT HACK

How to send email to users who haven't referred a customer yet

THE PHASE:
Scale

DIFFICULTY:
Advanced

WE USE:
Analytics + Email

The Hack:No matter how great the functionality your app. No matter how amazing its UX. No matter the customer support that comes attached to your subscription plan. Regardless of any other positives that your product may possess. Some users just won't refer their friends. Or they may take such a long time to refer someone that you know there must be some way to get them to do so sooner. Obviously, your goal is to get them to take action as soon as possible. Here's how to hack email referrals.

Now Hack It:

- For this hack to work, you need to have some way of tracking referrals.

- This can be achieved by using apps such as KISSmetrics, Mixpanel, or even Google Analytics if configured properly.

- You then need to configure your transactional email app such as Mandrill, SendGrid. Or Mailgun to send out an automated email if the user hasn't referred anyone after a certain period of time.

- You can also use apps such as Autosend.io to achieve similar lifecycle marketing functionality.

- The email can contain something along the lines of:
  - Thanks for using our app
  - This email contains a promo code that gives you and a friend a free month of our …
  - Let us know if you want more promo codes and we'd be happy to send these.

- The message needn't be complex. What's important is that it is much more personal than just providing a "Share with a Friend" link, which NO ONE responds to.

- The goal is to automate the process so that users who are on the fence about referring someone will start doing so.

83

THE GROWTH CULTURE HACK RE HACK

How to make your website content personal

THE PHASE:
Scale

DIFFICULTY:
Intermediate

WE USE:
Growthhackers.
com has a
new product
called Canvas
that's perfect
for tracking
experiments

The Hack: Many companies like to think they are capable of growth hacking, but in the plain light of day they're not. The traditional corporate culture doesn't support growth hacking, and without improvement, would likely fail at any experimental initiatives.

Why's that you say? Here are a few reasons:

Growth hacking is a cross-functional challenge, and most corporations aren't prepared for the amount of collaboration and data sharing between functions necessary for integrated growth. Most companies keep data siloed and don't share (think FBI vs. CIA).

Experimentation is an exercise in failure, as typically eight out of ten experiments aren't materially successful. Corporations aren't traditionally adept at dealing with failures and having the commitment to the process to wait out the successes. It's an instant gratification culture set.

Lastly, growth hacking searches for new channels and opportunities, and often these channels threaten the status quo. When growth relies on employees innovating themselves out of a job, it's rarely successful.

Here are some ideas you can use to create a culture of experimentation

Now Hack It:

- Keep a list of experiments that make you curious and invite every employee to add to it.

- Prioritize the list every month so the most important, high potential experiments rise to the top.

- Determine your experimentation velocity. How often will you run each type of experiment? Make this into a routine and your experimentation will skyrocket.

- Define the experiment properly, so you know what you're looking for. Write down your hypothesis, expected results and what KPIs you'll track. If you have no KPIs you'll never know if it was a success or a failure.

- Use a tracking spreadsheet to track your results. We use a system called PILLARS (stands for Place, Idea, Labor, Link, Audience, Results, Spend).Or you can try Canvas from GrowthHackers.com for a cool tracking system.

PRO TIP:
You can test different experiments at different intervals at the same time. For example, you may need two weeks of data to test an audience but only one week to test creative

84

THE TRIGGER HACK

How to implement automatic trigger based emails

THE PHASE:
Scale

DIFFICULTY:
Advanced

WE USE:
Customer.io (free to start, then $50/ month and up)

The Hack: Email automation is easy to do but difficult to do well. Tons of providers promise customers email nirvana and then screw them with limitations or technical requirements beyond our abilities.

We were introduced to a company called Customer.io and we're very impressed with their philosophies on email marketing. They allow marketers to basically segment "on the fly" and send automated emails to website visitors, based on pages they visit or actions they take.

While most email providers rely on segmentation on the back end, customer.io lets you link email messages to very specific front end actions. Give it a try, it's worth the time investment.

Now Hack It:

- Head over to customer.io and sign up for an account. You will install a small code snippet on your website to send data to customer.io.

- Follow the instructions to authenticate your domain and this will help increase your deliverability.

- Create your first segment. Experiment a lot and be creative. You can set up a segment for people who visit your "pricing page" or for people who download a whitepaper.

- Create your first campaign. Create an email and determine which segment should receive it and when.

- Test your campaign. Never launch a rule until you're confident that it is working properly.

PRO TIP:
Combine your newly learned email trigger ninja skills with your new drip email campaign knowledge for a steroid era email marketing platform!

85

THE USER COLLABORATION HACK

How to collaborate with users on product development

THE PHASE:
Scale

DIFFICULTY:
Intermediate

WE USE:
Many apps
available

The Hack: When was the last time you got your users involved in shaping your product? No, really involved? We're not talking about quickly throwing something on UserTesting.com before pushing your new feature to production.

We're talking about actually building something from the ground up in close collaboration with your current or future customers. You know, the REAL lean start-up way of building a product. If you're being honest with yourself then you realize there may have been some shortcuts taken on the road to attaining true "leanness."

If, after doing a fair amount of soul-searching, you can still say hand-on-heart that you've actually followed the lean approach to a T. Then we salute you!

For the rest of us growth h4x0rz, read on to find out how to create better products by getting your users involved from the outset.

Now Hack It:

- Before you start entertaining the idea of creating an app – any app – you need to find out that there's actual demand for it. How? By getting your users involved in its development.

- Even if you're just looking at implementing a new feature, ensure your users are involved! This is best achieved by iterating on bare-bones prototypes while getting constant feedback and input from your users.

- ProductHunt have used Invision for prototyping their iOS app. However, there are a huge number of prototyping tools available. Pick the one that works best for your situation.

- For creating new features, you can get users involved by running in-app surveys using tools such as Apptentive and others.

- Also, don't forget about good old email replies and encourage these in your communications with a user.

- There's no better way to retain a user than to have them co-create a product with you or make them aware that their voice is heard.

- Don't "masturcreate" a product in isolation. Find willing partners and start doing some serious app baby-making together!

86

THE SIDEKICK SITE PAGES HACK

How to create site pages for organic traffic nirvana

THE PHASE:
Scale

DIFFICULTY:
Intermediate

WE USE:
Content production horsepower and Buzzsumo.com for research

The Hack: While interviewing Anum Hussain for her case study on the growth of Sidekick, she brought up a growth hack that we thought was so powerful that it deserved its own growth hack. So this one's for you Anum!

It's always good to have a growth role model or a company that you watch for inspiration and ideas. Anum had her eye on the resource pages published by Helpscout.com - they were able to rank these content-heavy pages really well on Google search engine results pages, and even outranked Wikipedia on the search for "customer acquisition."

Knowing how hard it is to outrank Wikipedia, Anum realized that Help Scout was onto something and created six site pages of her own - pages on key search keywords with tons of customer-centric copy aggregated onto single resource pages.

And her organic traffic increased week over week by more than 10% (or in other words, she doubled her organic traffic every six weeks!)

Now Hack It:

- Find your own growth role model with one of Sidekick's site pages: http://www.getsidekick.com/email-etiquette-tips

- Aggregate all your topical content in one place.

- Update all your previous blog posts on the topic to include prominent links to the site pages for increased organic traffic to both the new and the original post.

- Remember the 80/20 rule applies to content - 20% of your pages, posts and content are going to generate 80% of your organic traffic, so treat them differently.

- Double down on topics and posts that are working the best by reformatting them and including them on site pages.

87

THE SOCIAL MENTIONS HACK

How to track and follow up with social media mentions

THE PHASE:
Scale

DIFFICULTY:
Intermediate

WE USE:
Try mention.com
(free to try, than
$29/month
and up)

The Hack: A lot of the challenge of growth hacker marketing is to learn how to identify customers right in the key moment where they're primed to make a decision.

The truth of the matter is that it's bloody hard to do. Search engine marketing is so explosive (and expensive) because search is the best known way to determine what an online buyer's intent is.

Social media offers the promise to catch customers in that moment. If you're a roofer and someone in your area posts on Facebook about a roof leak, you should say hi. If you're a mortgage broker and someone in your area tweets that they're looking at new houses this weekend, they're in the moment.

Bottom line - pay attention to what people are saying about you or your industry on social media and be prepared to respond quickly if you find customers in their a-ha moment.

Now Hack It:

- Create a new account at mention.com.

- Set up your mentions - your brand name, competitors, queries you want to track, etc.

- Get notified whenever the mention happens and follow-up directly through the dashboard.

PRO TIP:
You can test different experiments at different intervals at the same time. For example, you may need two weeks of data to test an audience but only one week to test creative

88

THE 'LET'S START A T-SHIRT BUSINESS' HACK

How to hack a t-shirt business that never touches a t-shirt

THE PHASE:
Launch

DIFFICULTY:
Intermediate

WE USE:
Shopify.com,
thePrintful.com

The Hack: Are you currently reading this book strapped to a corporate office desk and secretly yearning to have a start-up of your own? It's actually a really good idea. Having a small side project will give you a "petri dish" to experiment with and apply your new skills to.

The technology has never been easier to use and more accessible than it is now. And the barriers to entry have never been lower. So what are you waiting for?

This hack uses an example of a t-shirt business to show how e-commerce technology can be leveraged to launch a business quickly and cheaply, and never have to worry about the four killers for most product businesses and distributors: inventory, manufacturing, fulfillment and shipping.

Pick a niche (based on your passions and your keyword research to confirm enough monthly search volume), bootstrap some great designs and start supplementing that income!

Now Hack It:

- Find a starting point. Combine good search volume, reachability of audience, competitiveness and design potential to make your decision. Pick a niche you're passionate about and make it fun!

- Refer to the hacks on graphic design to get your designs made cheaply. Your budget will determine which is the best service to create your designs with.

- Refer to the previous hack on how to launch a Shopify store.

- Head over to the Shopify app store and sign up for Printful. This service will integrate with your Shopify inventory and create t-shirts on their platform. These t-shirts can be printed on demand to order, and fulfilled remotely, so you never see a t-shirt and you never see a packing slip.

- Every time a customer orders a shirt, the order goes to Printful for manufacturing and fulfillment. They'll take the cost of the shirt out of your account and deposit the sales revenue. You keep the difference!

PRO TIP:
Shopify has created an amazing video that goes step-by-step through this process. If you want to give e-commerce a shot, check it out here: https://www.youtube.com/watch?v=Z0yhS_sJkMk

89

THE HUBSPOT HACK

How to make Hubspot your digital marketing ground zero

THE PHASE:
Scale

DIFFICULTY:
Advanced

WE USE:
Husbpot.com

marketing.grader.
com

academy.hubspot.
com

library.hubspot.
com

The Hack: At some point, you're going to have enough consistent, predictable revenue growth that you're going to need to improve your marketing stack. The bootstrapped systems and processes you put in place will have limitations, and won't be able to perform to the degree you need it to.

Who you going to call? Ghostbusters? You could but you'll get an annoying out of business tone. Do the smart thing and call Hubspot.

Hubspot is a marketing platform that lets you build all your inbound marketing functions into one platform. Think blogging, SEO, CRM, landing pages, automation, calls to action, and analytics all in one place.

With start-ups focused on acquisition and managing every dollar, Hubspot is traditionally too expensive for start-up marketers who look enviously at their Hubspot-enabled colleagues. But when the time comes, Hubspot can become the enterprise software for your marketing department, and can save you tons of money in the long run.

Setting up Hubspot is complex if you're going to leverage all its functionality, so we won't explain how to get set-up, make them work for your money and besides it's part of the package. They have a great customer success team that will help you out so you learn how to use the system.

As a first step take a look at some of the free resources provided by Hubspot, which will help you learn inbound marketing and improve your marketing process, regardless if you're ready to invest in Hubspot.

Now Hack It:

- Not only does Hubspot have great software, they have amazing free resources and tools to become a kick ass Inbound marketer.

- A cool place to start is marketing.grader.com - enter your company URL and your email address to receive a free marketing report that grades your marketing efforts in several categories. A great tool for knowing where to start your improvements.

- Next check out their library resources at library.hubspot.com. Here you'll find an unprecedented amount of high quality videos and resources. Filter for the challenges you're currently working on, and you'll find great resources to supercharge your efforts.

- Lastly, head over to the academy, the jewel of the Hubspot resource hub. Read and watch a ton of good content or, better yet, get yourself Inbound Certified for free (an intensive course that is respected by many hiring marketing managers).

PRO TIP:
Are you a start-up at one of hundreds of accelerators or incubators across the continent? **If so, Hubspot's Jumpstart program allows you to access Hubspot for 95% off the regular price!** Head over to http://www.hubspot.com/jumpstart and see if you qualify.

CASE STUDY #9
BRIAN
CRISTIANO
CO-FOUNDER
OF BOLD
WORLDWIDE

Say No to FOMO

Bold Worldwide is a New York based ad agency, specializing in sports and lifestyle brands – both the sports brands and the lifestyle brands that want to attract the sports fans. Over time, Bold Worldwide has become one of the biggest sports focused ad agencies in the country, serving clients from Gillette to Pepsi and from the New York Mets to NASCAR. Founder and CEO Brian Cristiano has made several strategic decisions along the way that lead directly to their growth and status in the industry.

Brian began his adventure in 2001, when he founded a video production company that produced high end videos for agencies. The ad agencies would hire them when their clients needed video, so the production company never dealt directly with clients. The company had 12 employees and a number of contract freelancers, when the 2008 recession hit, leaving ad agencies the victim of the slashed marketing budgets.

Play The Long Game

With that economic climate in mind, Brian's first pivot came in 2009, when he decided to go direct to client, and basically cut out the ad agency middlemen that were marking up their work and selling to clients. Brian set a goal of replacing his production company revenue within a year, by changing their focus from agencies to brands and marketers. Bold succeeded in attracting these direct customers in two ways; firstly, they maintained relationships with the clients they worked for indirectly, and let them know that they could engage directly and save time and money on the videos. Secondly, Brian used conferences and trade shows to target medium sized advertisers who weren't the focus of the big Madison Avenue agencies. His secret was to do much of the research work before hand, schmoozing conference organizers into giving him the exhibitor lists and connecting on LinkedIn long before the show. .As a result Brian was able to replace all his agency based revenue within 18 months, and now had a flourishing direct to client business.

Say No to FOMO

Brian's next pivot came in 2012.Frustrated with the lack of synergy between his industries of expertise, Brian became frustrated with having to learn a new client industry from scratch and felt that it took them longer to "hit the ground running" then he wanted. Through a period of research (where was their opportunity) and internal soul-searching (what are we best at), Brian came to the conclusion that if he would focus on the sports vertical, he could attract new clients based on his vertical expertise, and could help non-competing clients learn from each other. .Brian also loved the fact that his research showed that he'd be competing with a small handful of sports-focused agencies as opposed to 1500 big, traditional agencies.

The "a-ha moment" came when "the business development vibe changed completely", explained Brian, ".And the results followed – Brian was quickly able to replace all the non-sports clients with sports clients, based mainly on industry specific case studies, leveraging other successful sports work and through client referrals to non-competing clients in the sports world.

Focus and then Focus some more.

Not satisfied, Brian turned the lens internally and really asked the hard questions to figure out what specific services they were the best at, what services were the most profitable for them, what services could be leverage their learning universally across clients and where the future of marketing was heading. All the signs pointed to a mainly digital strategy, focused on digital media, social media, online storytelling and brand building. Brian "reverse engineered" what his business would look like at scale (200 or 400 employees), shuddered low performing/low margin departments and focused on the digital departments. That way they could focus on work that clients loved, had high margins, would have a faster sales cycle and was easiest to replicate without sacrificing quality or margins.

Bold Worldwide is now one of the top digital sports marketing agencies in the world, due in large part to Brian's strategic pivots and asking a lot of hard questions.

So what would Brian like marketers to learn from Bold's experiences?

Firstly, Brian says that specialization is the key to growth and scale. Pick an industry you're good at, choose services you're the best at, and focus on being the best in class to clients that make the most sense for your business. There is so much competition in the agency space, that focusing allows you to better attract industry clients who expect their agency to understand their industry as table stakes.

Secondly, say no to FOMO (fear of missing out).What this means is that most entrepreneurs are terrified of the thought of turning down perfectly good business by focusing on a specific niche. Brian says that by focusing on the clients and services that are most strategic for you, you can do better work and generate higher margins. In a highly niched world, being the best to a targeted group of companies is the only option and being "everything to everyone" is no longer a viable strategy. The fear of missing out causes many very intelligent leaders to turn down focused, scalable strategies in favor of generalized, wide reaching strategies that rarely resonate with the typical advertising clients.

Finally, the real benefit of specialization is that you can reduce the learning cycle by specializing on industry and service, so that you constantly get better and your learnings can be applied directly across all clients. This allows for a more efficient delivery of service, a higher quality product and more satisfied customers, leading to more client referrals. Once Brian focused on digital services, he was able to speed up the learning curve with each new client, and show them very focused examples and case studies in their industry, that they could easily relate to and understand.

PERSONAL PRODUCTIVITY HACKS

What kind of a Guide would this be if we didn't include a bonus section!?

So enjoy this collection of personal productivity hacks that we like to use to make our lives easier and give us the freedom to daydream new growth hacks!

Some of the ideas in this section have saved us hours of time, and really allow us to focus on our funnels.

We hope you enjoy!

90

THE PERSONAL ASSISTANT HACK

How to have your own personal assistant without breaking the bank

THE PHASE:
Launch

DIFFICULTY:
Beginner

WE USE:
FancyHands.com
(packages start
at $29.99/month
for 5 requests,
requests rollover
to the next month
if unused)

The Hack: Wouldn't it be nice to have a personal assistant? Someone to help us get organized, keep us focused and productive, and handle tasks that pull us off the bill paying jobs and require our time to be spent somewhere else?

Not only is it expensive to hire a personal assistant, finding a good one is tough. It's also tough to keep them busy for 40 hours a week.

We use a service called Fancy Hands to help make our lives a little bit easier. With Fancy Hands, you subscribe to a monthly number of requests, which can be used for completing personal tasks.

Tasks can include meeting scheduling (right into your Google calendar), online shopping, managing travel itineraries, research and they can even call your cable company to make sure you're on the best cable package!

Now that's what we call productivity.

Now Hack It:

- Sign-up for Fancy Hands using your Facebook account. It makes it easier down the road.

- Select the number of requests you think you'll need a month. Start with a lower package until you know how much you'll use it.

- Install the mobile app. Not only is it the easiest way to submit a request, you can use the microphone and dictate the request to your assistant.

- Your assistant will do your dirty work and get back to you really quickly, usually within a few hours.

PRO TIP:
Want Fancy Hands to schedule meetings for you? Set up Personal Touch. Create a corporate email address for your personal assistant and register the email address with Fancy Hands. When they email your colleagues to schedule meetings, it will come from that dedicated email, and will look like a real person (regardless of which assistant responds to your request)!

THE MARKET RESEARCH HACK

How to outsource your market research overseas

THE PHASE:
Any time

DIFFICULTY:
Beginner

WE USE:
Many companies exist but we like www.acelerartech.com

The Hack: Want to know what sheer pleasure it is to a growth hacker? Assign a research project before you go to sleep and wake up to the results! Hit the ground running when you head into the office, knowing that you've made sleeping productive!

This is possible. We have used overseas assistants for many tasks including research, graphic design and data entry to name a few.

The key to efficiently manage your overseas service provider is communication - communicate very simply, clearly and literally. Give examples and templates for your expectations. And develop a relationship with your assistants. Putting in the effort at the beginning will save all the hassle with unnecessary re-work.

Now Hack It:

- Research the overseas companies that are offering virtual assistant and research services. Ask to speak to some of their customers as references.

- Develop a sample task for them to complete for you. Take a non-mission-critical task and pay them to complete it.

- Analyze the work. Was it done on time and on budget? And was the quality up to par?

- If you're not happy with the results, try again. If you are, then develop the relationship.

PRO TIP:
The prices overseas are obviously much lower than the prices we pay here. But don't be greedy or cheap. There are differences in service quality between the various prices. Pay a little more and you'll get a great quality output, for a fraction of the local price. Remember the adage that ""if you pay with peanuts, you get monkeys"

92

THE GRAPHIC DESIGN HACK

How to hack your graphic design (for all budgets)

THE PHASE:
Launch

DIFFICULTY:
Intermediate

WE USE:
Fiverr.com (logos from $5)

99designs.com (logos from $299)

canva.com (free)

The Hack: Graphic design is a pain for the entrepreneur.

You always need it, you can rarely afford to pay for it, and it needs to be GREAT if you're going to be a successful growth hacker. It really is one of those non-negotiable tasks.

In the past, graphic design was hugely fragmented and expensive and if you're looking in the wrong place it still can be today. However, over the past five years, there has been so much innovation in the graphic design space, that the growth hacker now has a number of quick, cheap options to get the designs they need.

Not only is this awesome but it further reduces the barriers to entry for today's digital marketers and entrepreneurs.

Being able to create your own graphics is extremely empowering. Invest some time in becoming proficient. Many great options exist depending on your budget, such as the following:

Now Hack It:

- If you're on the tightest of budgets and poor on time to get to learning then Fiverr.com is for you. It is a marketplace of graphic designers, who will create graphics for you for as low as $5.Quality varies greatly, so use the reviews and recommendations to narrow down your search. For a small additional payment, you can get same day graphics delivery!

- If you have a little more to spend, but not enough to hire a design agency, then head over to 99designs.com and create a design competition. Pick the category you need created and decide how much you want to spend on your contest. The more you spend, the more response you'll receive. Fill out the design brief, launch your contest and wait for the submissions to arrive. You only pay if you find one you like. Feedback is the key, so give great feedback to the designers you like the best.

- Want to learn to make amazing graphics by yourself? It's never been this easy. Create a free account at Canva.com. There you'll have access to thousands of gorgeous design templates where you can upload your own imagery or use theirs for $1/photo. Warning–this can be addictive to the designer trapped inside your body. They have also expanded their offer to allow you to create a "branding" portfolio for your business so you can get letterheads and proposals looking sharp.

PRO TIP:
Need something a little less hacky? Head over to the designers at dribbble.com and browse their work. If you see someone you like, reach out to the designer and hire them to help.

93

THE 'TO THE CLOUD' HACK

How to manage all your files in the cloud

THE PHASE:
Launch

DIFFICULTY:
Beginner

WE USE:
Dropbox.com

Drive.Google.com

iCloud.com

The Hack: The days of managing your files locally are thankfully coming to an end. The best way to keep your documents shareable, backed up and accessible from any device is to store them in the cloud using any of the popular cloud storage services available today.

Once stored, you can share them through share links and collaborate on them remotely without worrying about version control or security. They are now backed up, so when you spill Red Bull on your keyboard, your most important files will be safe. And you can access them from anywhere, including pretty nifty mobile apps on your smartphones.

With storage costs bordering on free, there's no excuse for being unorganized or not backed up. Let's do this.

Now Hack It:

- It's very straightforward.
- Create your cloud storage account.
- Create the folder structure that makes sense for you.
- Upload your local files to the appropriate drives.
- Sleep well knowing you're backed up.
- You can set up automatic backups to keep your files synced with the cloud account. Try to only select the most important folders to backup, this will avoid backing up useless data.

PRO TIP:
In Google Drive, there are several ways to share a file. You can input the email addresses of the people who can view it, in either "read only" or "can edit" mode. You can also set the link so anyone who has the link can view it. Lastly, you can make it completely private..

94

THE BUSINESS TRAVEL HACK

How to hack your business travel

THE PHASE:
Any time

DIFFICULTY:
Beginner

WE USE:
https://www.tripit.com/

airbnb.com/business-travel
expensify.com

The Hack: Business travel for most is a necessary evil of work. It's exhausting, time consuming, expensive and requires a lot of focus to stay organized and accounted for.

Use these business travel hacks to save money, save time, make travel easier or just to make travel a little more fun and comfortable.

We look forward to a day when business travel is a thing of the past. Until then, hack away and travel safely. Don't talk to strangers, unless they're cute.

Now Hack It:

- Tripit is an app that allows you to keep your itinerary information all in one place. What's even cooler is you simply forward your travel confirmation email (hotel, airline, transportation, restaurants etc.) to your Tripit email, and it organizes it into an itinerary for you! Virtual PA stuff of the future, today!

- Airbnb recently launched a service for businesses that enables employees to book Airbnb locations instead of hotel rooms, and charge them to a master account. Many travelers are preferring the creature comforts of a nice Airbnb over a hotel room, and companies can save significant cost by avoiding bloated conference hotel prices. A win-win!

- Lastly, if you hate keeping track of your expenses on the road, use an app like Expensify, which takes the pain out of tracking, documenting and reporting your expenses.

PRO TIP:
Want to be an airport Ninja? Register for Nexus/Global entry if you fly internationally, take only carry on whenever possible (use hotel dry cleaning instead) and grab a taxi from departure level instead of the busy arrival level. You'll be home in no time.

95

THE TIME SAVER HACK

How to use textexpander to save time every single day

THE PHASE:
Launch

DIFFICULTY:
Beginner

WE USE:
https://chrome.
google.com/
webstore/detail/
auto-text-ex-
pander-for-go/
iibninhmiggehl-
cdolcilmhacigh-
jamp?hl=en

The Hack: If you're like us, you type the same things over and over

Get yourself a text expander website browser add-on and set up your own shortcodes for things like email addresses, company names, websites, physical addresses, phone numbers and other common phrases.

By creating and learning these codes, you can save yourself time and hassle and make typing very quick.

Now Hack It:

- Go to the Chrome app store.

- Select and install a text expander app.

- Populate the app with your most commonly typed phrases, email addresses, etc.

- Use the short codes and save time.

PRO TIP:
Install the app in your website's navigation bar, and instead of memorizing short-codes, you can click them from a list of your customized codes.

96

THE PRODUCT DEMO HACK

How to create great product demo photos

THE PHASE:
Launch

DIFFICULTY:
Beginner

WE USE:
PlaceIt.net
(single photos
and subscriptions
are available)

The Hack: One thing all growth hackers need are great photos, especially product photos for demos or e-commerce sales.

Most photos suck - they are cut out of their native backgrounds and placed on a stark white background, and always seem to have that DIY feel to them, which frankly only creates a serious feel of the amateur.

PlaceIt has made it easy for product marketers (particularly app or web service marketers) to create amazing high res photos of their products or services, superimposed onto mobile device or computer screens for "in situ" imagery. Believe me, if you're thinking "Photoshop can do that" you'll be in a world of hurt when you pass this one up for the granddaddy of image manipulation, unless you've spent the last few years of your life studying the ways of Adobe.

These images look great on product pages, demo pages and anywhere else you want to show off your digital product in action. Drag and drop image creation makes it easy and intuitive for anyone to use.

Now Hack It:

- Head over to PlaceIt.net and start browsing their catalog of template photos.

- When you find one you like, select it and you'll be prompted to enter your product photo. You can upload a photo or even add a screenshot simply by entering the URL!

- And any text or effects you want and download the photo.

PRO TIP:
PlaceIt also supports video, so you can have your product video playing on the subject's screen. That'll be taking it to the next level!

97

THE OFFLINE
READER HACK

How to use Pocket to create
your own growth hacking hub

THE PHASE:
Launch

DIFFICULTY:
Beginner

WE USE:
getpocket.com
(free)

The Hack: If you take our advice, you'll start spending a lot of time learning. You'll read a lot of blog posts, articles, websites and books to stay on the cutting edge of marketing. If you're not, you're doing it wrong!

A great way to keep your articles organized and available to read is by using Pocket as your article reader.

Pocket lets you bookmark and categorize articles for future reading. It also makes it really easy to bookmark the pages. Offline reading features create a growth hacking learning hub you can read anywhere.

Now Hack It:

- Sign up for a free account at getpocket.com.

- Download the pocket mobile app for your smartphone. This allows you to read your saved articles anywhere.

- Add the Pocket "bookmarklet" by following the instructions at sign-up. This creates a little button on your desktop or laptop browser that will automatically send articles you're reading online to your pocket account.

- Add Pocket as your "offline reader" on your social media sites. For example, by making Pocket your offline reader on Twitter, it adds a bookmark option right in the Twitter app. Just press and hold the link you want to save, and you'll get a "send to Pocket" option.

PRO TIP:
If you really enjoy the articles you're saving to Pocket, why not curate a personal weekly newsletter and send it out to your followers? Use a service like paper.li to take your stores links and turn them into a shareable digest. Genius right

98

THE EVERNOTE HACK

How to use Evernote to supercharge your productivity

THE PHASE:
Anytime

DIFFICULTY:
Beginner

WE USE:
Evernote.com
(free)

The Hack: Evernote is everyone's favorite tool for collecting notes from around the web and keeping them organized in one place. It works across just about every device you can imagine and even has a cool app for Chrome called Web Clipper.

With a range of account options from free up to business, there is a plan suited for everyone. Once you've got yourself signed up you'll wonder how you ever lived without it. Being organized is like half the battle of daily life.

Here are some tips to supercharge your Evernote use and stay as organized as possible.

Now Hack It:

- Keep groups of notes related and accessible by creating a table of contents. Select the notes you want to include and click "create table of contents notes." This will create a clickable table of contents.

- Add Evernote's "quick note bar" to your iPhone's home screen for quick note creation. Ensure "access to lock screen" is enabled and then edit the notification center settings to include Evernote.

- If you're on your iPhone and browsing a webpage you want to save as a note, tap the Share button and select Evernote.

- Use the keyboard shortcut Command-J to jump between notebooks quickly.

PRO TIP:
Did you know you can email content into your Evernote account? Simply locate your Evernote email address in the settings page and send your content to that email address. Voila!

99

THE SUPER NETWORKER HACK

How to use Newsle to keep in touch with your network

THE PHASE:
Any time

DIFFICULTY:
Beginner

WE USE:
Newsle.com

The Hack: Keeping in touch with your network is really important as you don't want to be seen as someone who only reaches out when they need something. Seriously you don't want to be one of those friends.

Sign up with Newsle (purchased by LinkedIn in 2014) and they will send you emails every time there's a news story about someone in your network. That way you can email them with a congratulations on their new product launch or promotion.

Choose to have the news stories emailed to you as they happen or in a handy weekly digest. Network away.

258 — THE GROWTH HACKERS GUIDE TO THE GALAXY

Now Hack It:

- Head over to Newsle.com and sign up with your LinkedIn account.

- Newsle will import your LinkedIn contacts and ask if you'd like to import from email to? If you have Gmail, the import is really easy.

- You'll be taken to a feed of all the articles your network has been featured in recently. You'll also get a separate feed with journalists and celebrity articles.

- Now head over to "settings" and tell Newsle how often you want to be notified by email.

PRO TIP:
It's better to give than to receive (That's what she said). If someone has a new job and you know someone great to introduce him to in their new industry, that's a great way to follow up on the Newsle news (and add value to that contact).

100

THE LIFETIME ACHIEVEMENT HACK

How to live a life of constant learning

THE PHASE:
Any time

DIFFICULTY:
Advanced

WE USE:
Our Superior
Intellect and
Ability To Keep
Our Finger On
The Pulse

The Hack: If you've gotten this far we're sure you agree with us by now that growth hacking is as much about the mindset as it is about the individual tools in your growth hacking toolkit. And it's been made pretty clear that you no longer need to be a programmer to be able to growth hack to great success.

Remember though, the battlefield changes daily, and the tools that were popular six months ago could be obsolete by now, just like every other piece of technology known to man. So it's your job, young growth hacker, to commit yourself to ABL - "always be learning."

In order to send you off with the resources you need, this final growth hack will show you where to go, who to follow and what to read to keep your mind sharp and skills up-to-date.

Now Hack It:

- Communities are the easiest way to feel the pulse of the growth hacking industry. Being active in these communities will expose you to great thought leadership, let you ask questions and meet great digital marketers. Don't treat it as a one way street, it's all about the art of sharing. Ain't nobody got time for people who are only around to take others ideas. Check out these communities to get involved:

- Inbound.org
- GrowthHackers.com
- WarriorForum.com
- GrowthHacker.tv

- The most up to date marketing content is usually found in the blog posts of our thought leaders. The easiest way to stay current is to read the best marketing blogs out there, which include:
  - Sean Ellis http://www.startup-marketing.com/
  - Lincoln Murphy http://lincolnmurphy.com/
  - Neil Patel http://neilpatel.com/
  - Noah Kagan http://okdork.com/
  - Sujan Patel http://sujanpatel.com/
  - Brian Balfour http://www.coelevate.com/
  - Dharmesh Shaw http://blog.hubspot.com/marketing/author/dharmesh-shah
  - Jim Grey https://grayj.co/

- There are shizit loads of great books that can help a growth hacker think differently. Here are a few of our favorites:
  - "Traction" by Gabriel Weinberg and Justin Mares
  - "Lean Analytics" by Alistair Croll and Ben Yoskovitz
  - "Start-up Owner's Manual" by Steve Blank
  - "Value Proposition Design and Business Model Generation" by Alex Osterwalder
  - "Hooked" by Nir Eyal
  - "Positioning: The Battle for your Mind" by Al Ries
  - "Running Lean" by Ash Maurya

- Over the last few years, a bunch of great conferences have emerged that are like all-you-can-eat buffets for marketers in terms of education and networking. Who doesn't like an all-you-can-eat?! Here are some you should check out if you have the chance:
  - Hubspot's Inbound Conference - www.inbound.com
  - Traction Conference - www.tractionconf.io
  - Mozcon by Moz - www.moz.com/mozcon
  - Unbounce's CTA Conference - www.calltoactionconf.com/
  - Conversion XL - live.conversionxl.com/

ABOUT THE AUTHORS

JEFF GOLDENBERG

Jeff Goldenberg is the Head of Growth at Borrowell, a leading Canadian online marketplace lender. He is a sought after expert and speaker in the areas of digital marketing, growth hacking and business development for innovative, high-growth companies.

He is an Entrepreneur-in-Residence at MaRS Discovery District as well as a mentor at the TechStars/Startup Next accelerator. Jeff lives in Toronto with his wife Sage and his son Jackson.

Find him at www.jeffgoldenberg.net and on Twitter @jeff_goldenberg

MARK HAYES

Mark Hayes is the founder of digital marketing consultancy, Rocketshp. Previously, Mark founded one of the world's first growth hacking agencies and has been mentioned in Wired UK, Forbes and The Wall Street Journal. Having worked client-side prior to starting Rocketshp, Mark knows how easy it is to go through a marketing budget without seeing many tangible results.

Being a marketer with a knack for the technical, he came across growth hacking years ago and was blown away by the results it helped to achieve. He has since fully embraced growth hacking strategies and advocates the use of these for his clients.

Mark believes that growth hacking is not just a buzzword but a different and more efficient way of approaching digital marketing. In his eyes, it is as much a mindset as it is a marketing discipline.

Mark is based in Auckland, New Zealand.

You can find Mark at https://rocketshp.com

WANT MORE?

FOR BLOG POSTS, VIDEO WALKTHROUGHS, GROWTH
HACKER GEAR OR TO HEAR THE GROWTH HACKER'S
GUIDE TO THE GALAXY PODCAST, VISIT
WWW.GROWTHHACKERGUIDE.COM

SOURCES AND INSPIRATION

HACK	SOURCE OR INSPIRATION
2	https://community.unbounce.com/unbounce/topics/how-can-i-create-a-youtube-video-background?_ga=1.179650084.1456567854.1428937684
6	http://technicalmarketing.io/cro/saas-pricing-technique-decoy-effect/
14	Source: Nick Eubanks as seonick.net
19	http://sixteenventures.com/saas-growth-hacking-email
22	https://www.groovehq.com/blog/early-wins
	http://blog.forkly.com/a-viral-launching-soon-form/
23	https://pippinsplugins.com/products/love-it-pro-for-wordpress/
24	http://blog.leadpages.net/free-download-tap-word-mouth-marketing-invite-friend-thank-page/
25	https://custdevlabs.wordpress.com/2013/09/24/google-news-api-mturk-press/
26	http://www.growthhacking.biz/6-great-hacks-for-user-growth/
29	https://www.growthhacker.tv/recipes/?id=1362
30	http://blog.statuspage.io/how-we-increased-our-conversion-rate-by-311-percent
31	http://growtheverywhere.com/inspiration/backlinko-brian-dean-build-traffic-seo
32	http://pando.com/2014/01/16/3-startups-that-launched-without-writing-code/
33	http://unbounce.com/landing-pages/checklist
34	http://blog.ghost.org/ghost-onboarding
46	Wordstream.com

SOURCES AND INSPIRATION

HACK	SOURCE OR INSPIRATION
51	http://blog.idonethis.com/first-5000-users/
	http://giantbatfarts.com/story/reddit_how
52	http://andrisatteka.blogspot.co.nz/2014/10/creepy-visitor-tracking-using-linkedin.html
	http://blog.makensi.es/post/3679713636/fingerprinting-your-visitors-using-social-networks
53	http://techcrunch.com/2014/10/22/spot-im
56	http://mixergy.com/course-cheat-sheet-growth-hacking-2
57	http://ivankreimer.com/buffer-revenue-dashboard/
	https://open.bufferapp.com/buffer-public-revenue-dashboard/
60	100 Days of Growth
61	http://southernweb.com/2013/04/how-video-transcription-can-help-seo/
63	http://www.programmingformarketers.com/lesson-1-viral-referral-campaigns/
64	http://okdork.com/2014/06/18/the-samuel-l-jackson-marketing-hack/
66	https://blog.captainup.com/engaging-website-design-5-unpredictability/
	http://andrewchen.co/easter-egg-marketing-how-snapchat-apple-and-google-hook-you/
69	http://blog.sendwithus.com/measuring-nps-with-wufoo-and-free-survey-templates/friend or colleague?
70	http://www.wsj.com/news/articles/SB10001424052702304500404579129590411867328 https://www.facebook.com/photo.php?v=75505423022

SOURCES AND INSPIRATION

HACK	SOURCE OR INSPIRATION
72	https://blog.kissmetrics.com/double-your-leads-instantly/
73	https://econsultancy.com/blog/64142-why-online-retailers-should-enclose-the-checkout-process/
	http://www.salecycle.com/cart-abandonment-stats/
74	https://github.com/carlsednaoui/ouibounce
	http://www.seoblog.com/2014/03/review-ouibounce-alternative-bounce-exchange
76	http://vimeo.com/72851585
	http://mashable.com/2013/05/03/contextual-marketing/
77	https://medium.com/@devonaedwards/uber-and-tripadvisors-click-to-uber-deal-fc891c7977b6
	http://e27.co/startup-marketing-101-the-art-of-strategic-partnerships-part-2-of-2/
78	http://readwrite.com/2010/09/05/6-saas-metrics-you-should-trac
80	http://www.saleshacker.com/lead-generation/sell-fortune-500-linkedin-hack/
82	http://growthhackingpro.com/4-must-email-growth-hacks-arent-using/app
83	https://medium.com/@kurtybot/pillars-a-system-im-using-to-track-my-crazy-growth-hacks-5ee0f9280f78
85	http://blog.leadpages.net/rise-product-hunt-5-growth-hacks-silicon-valleys-new-favorite-website
87	http://www.matthewbarby.com/saas-startup-growth-hacking/?utm_source=GrowthHackers.com&utm_medium=Community&utm_campaign=Submission#TrackFollow-uponBrandedMentions